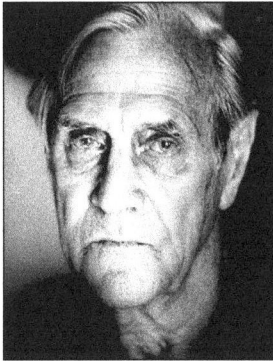

PATRICK WHITE (1912–90) was born in London but spent his early years in Australia. He studied in Australia and Cambridge, travelled widely, and served in Greece and the Middle East during the Second World War. He settled in Australia after the war and wrote many successful novels. He received a number of major awards including the 1973 Nobel Prize for Literature. His stage plays include *Return to Abyssinia* (1947), *The Ham Funeral* (1961), *The Season at Sarsaparilla* (produced 1962), *Night on Bald Mountain* (1964), *Big Toys* (1977), *Signal Driver* (1982), *Netherwood* (1983) and *Shepherd on the Rocks* (1987).

THE SEASON AT SARSAPARILLA

A charade of suburbia

Patrick White

CURRENCY PRESS
The performing arts publisher

CURRENCY PLAYS

First published in 1965
by Eyre and Spottiswoode, London, in *Four Plays*.
This edition published in 1965
by Currency Press Pty Ltd,
PO Box 2287, Strawberry Hills, NSW, 2012, Australia
enquiries@currency.com.au
www.currency.com.au

This edition published 2019

Cataloguing-in-publication data for this title is available from the National
Library of Australia website: www.nla.gov.au

Typeset by Dean Nottle for Currency Press.
Cover design by Lisa White.

NATIONAL LIBRARY OF AUSTRALIA

A catalogue record for this
book is available from the
National Library of Australia

Contents

Currency Press acknowledges the Traditional Owners of the Country on which we live and work. We pay our respects to all Aboriginal and Torres Strait Islander Elders, past and present.

The Season at Sarsaparilla was first produced by the Adelaide University Theatre Guild at the Union Theatre, Adelaide, on 14 September 1962, with the following cast:

JOYLEEN POGSON (PIPPY)	Elizabeth Steel
GIRLIE POGSON	Carmel Millhouse
DEEDREE	Bronwen Courtney
HARRY KNOTT	Wayne Anthoney
NOLA BOYLE	Zoe Caldwell
CLIVE POGSON	John Haynes
MAVIS KNOTT	Morna Jones
JUDY POGSON	Barbara West
ROY CHILD	Terence Stapleton
RON SUDDARDS	Don Barker
JULIA SHEEN	Barbara Dennis
ERNIE BOYLE	Cliff Neate
MR ERBAGE	Hedley Cullen
ROWLEY MASSON (DIGGER)	Leslie Dayman
FIRST AMBULANCE MAN	Ron Dix
SECOND AMBULANCE MAN	Albert Havard

Directed by John Tasker
Designed by Desmond Digby

CHARACTERS

HARRY KNOTT, in menswear

MAVIS KNOTT, his wife

ROY CHILD, her brother, a teacher

CLIVE POGSON, a business executive

GIRLIE POGSON, his wife

JUDY POGSON, his daughter, studying the violin

JOYLEEN (PIPPY), their little girl

DEEDREE, her little friend

ERNIE BOYLE, a sanitary man

NOLA BOYLE, his wife

ROWLEY MASSON (DIGGER), a mate

RON SUDDARDS, a post office clerk

JULIA SHEEN, a model

MR ERBAGE, an important person

TWO AMBULANCE MEN

SETTING

Mildred Street, Sarsaparilla, a fictitious outer suburb of Sydney, summer 1961.

ACT ONE

When the lights go up on the three homes in Mildred Street, there is an outburst of barking as from a pack of dogs somewhere in the distance. PIPPY POGSON *appears in the kitchen from one of the invisible rooms of the Pogson home, centre stage. A forthright and astute small girl. She runs through the kitchen, very determined, opens the invisible back door, pauses for a moment, looking and listening. She runs down the steps into the yard. Coming forward, she pulls open an invisible back gate. She is perhaps out to investigate the barking dogs. She stands at the gate (i.e. at the footlights) listening, shading her eyes, looking up and down the lane.* GIRLIE POGSON, *her mother, is heard calling from the front part of her house.*

GIRLIE: [*offstage, calling*] Pip-py …?! Pip-py?!

> PIPPY *scowls. She explodes under her breath, then runs and hides under the house. The barking continues spasmodically, gradually dying.* GIRLIE POGSON *enters her kitchen. A small, spruce woman in her forties. Not a hair out of place, and never will be. Everything must be nice, even if you pay the price.* MRS POGSON *wears all the marks of anxiety and a respectable social level.*

[*Calling, quite viciously by now, as she looks out of the back door*] Joy-leen!

> *She returns in despair into the kitchen.*

It's the holidays. It's the holidays. Always like this in the holidays. And now those dogs! It shouldn't be allowed.

> *Glancing at herself in a wall-mirror in passing, she corrects a hair, touches her frown, sighs. She goes out the back of the kitchen into the front part of her house. At the same time* DEEDREE *enters from the front garden. Slightly younger than her friend* PIPPY, *more innocent, easily put upon.* DEEDREE *is the eternal stooge. She is carrying two milk bottles, a loaf and a newspaper.*

DEEDREE: [*calling, tentatively*] Pip-py? Pip-py? Where are yer?

>   PIPPY *sticks her head out from under the house.*

PIPPY: [*scowling*] I'm here. Gee, you're early, Deedree. Didn't you have your breakfast? Mum won't give you any if you haven't.

DEEDREE: 'Course I had me breakfast. Didn't you?

PIPPY: [*angrily*] No. Yes!

>   *She comes out from under the house.*

I wasn't hungry. But I had some to keep her quiet.

DEEDREE: Is she going crook?

PIPPY: Always.

DEEDREE: What about?

PIPPY: Oh, everything.

>   DEEDREE *just stands.*

Says I know too much.

DEEDREE: [*devotedly*] You do know an awful lot, Pippy.

PIPPY: Well, I can't help that. It just comes to me.

>   *During the foregoing,* GIRLIE POGSON *re-enters her kitchen, starting (in mime) to get the next round of breakfast.*

DEEDREE: Monica Jeffreys is gunna read through the dictionary.

PIPPY: [*contemptuously*] Monica Jeffreys! Sooky thing!

DEEDREE: She's got as far as B.

PIPPY: I don't have to read the dictionary.

DEEDREE: [*indicating the loaf, milk and paper which she is carrying*] What am I gunna do with these, Pippy?

PIPPY: [*jerking her head at the kitchen*] Give them to her. It'll sweeten her up.

DEEDREE: [*doubtfully*] Ah!

GIRLIE: [*calling back into the house*] If you're not careful, Clive, you'll miss the bus … and who's to blame …?

>   DEEDREE *has mounted the back steps.*

DEEDREE: [*at the kitchen door*] Mrs Pogson! It's me, Mrs Pogson! [*Simpering*] Always bright and early!

GIRLIE: That is something you need never tell me, dear.

>   *She comes and takes* DEEDREE'*s offering.*

But thank you, Deedree, all the same.

She glances out of the door and catches sight of PIPPY.

That is where you are, Pippy. Did you hear me call?

PIPPY: [*kicking the ground*] Yes.

GIRLIE: And why didn't you come?

PIPPY: I didn't feel like it.

GIRLIE: Ooh, you bold little girl! I'll tell your father, Joyleen. One day you'll catch it.

PIPPY: [*chanting*] One day, one day,
      I shall learn to fly.
      I'll pin little wings on me shoulders,
      And fly.

GIRLIE: Ooh, you are the rudest little girl! And 'my', not 'me', Joyleen.

DEEDREE *has a fit of the giggles.*

What's the matter with you, Deedree Inkpen?

DEEDREE: Oh, nothing, Mrs Pogson!

GIRLIE: Well, if it's nothing, there's every reason for controlling yourself. [*Looking out*] Now, you children, I don't want you running in and out, marking the lino. The holidays are always death to anybody's lino.

DEEDREE: Yes, Mrs Pogson!

PIPPY *sticks out her tongue as* GIRLIE *retreats into the kitchen to continue with the breakfast preparations. At the same time* HARRY KNOTT *comes into the Knott kitchen from the front part of the house. He is a young man, probably younger than he looks, but responsibilities have been thrust upon him early. He is wearing his business pants, well-pressed, and beautifully laundered white shirt. Arm-bands. There is nothing distinctive about him.*

HARRY: [*calling back into the house*] You stay there, dear. Take it easy. Can't afford to take any risks now that it's so close.

PIPPY: I'm glad you came, Deedree. There's such a lot to tell you.

DEEDREE: What, Pippy?

PIPPY: It's the dogs …

NOLA BOYLE *comes into her kitchen. In her forties, she is dressed in a chenille dressing-gown. Generous of figure. Tawny of head.*

A lioness. Stretching and yawning. The barking has begun again in the distance.

GIRLIE: [*calling*] Clive?! If it's congealed eggs you want …!

HARRY: [*calling to his invisible wife*] A nice, light-boiled egg. Won't be a jiffy, Mave.

DEEDREE: I seen the dogs, Pippy. At the bus stop.

PIPPY: That's where it always begins. At the bus stop.

> NOLA, *who has been searching for something, discovers it on a shelf. She proceeds to do her lips long and lovingly in a mirror.*

DEEDREE: [*to* PIPPY] But what's up with all these dogs?

PIPPY: There's a bitch in season.

DEEDREE: What's that?

PIPPY: She's on heat. See?

DEEDREE: What's that do?

PIPPY: That's when she gets interesting to dogs …

> CLIVE POGSON *enters the Pogson kitchen. Around fifty. A rather thick-set business bull—a minor one, but he will probably never know that. He takes the paper and sits at the table, ready for breakfast.*

CLIVE: [*ritually*] Eggs, eh?

> GIRLIE, *above answering him, puts a plate in front of him.* MAVIS KNOTT *enters her kitchen. She is very pregnant under her dressing-gown. A bit miserable and fretful, though normally she would be a placid, acceptant young woman. Neither pretty nor plain. The average, decent suburban wife.*

HARRY: Arr, now, Mavis, it doesn't cost much to be reasonable!

MAVIS: [*heavily*] I can't be reasonable, Harry, not when I listen to someone moving around in me own kitchen.

> *After some routine pottering, to uphold her rights, she sits and lets him serve her with breakfast.*

DEEDREE: [*still in the dark, to* PIPPY] And when she gets interesting?

> PIPPY *sticks her mouth in her friend's ear and explains very forcibly.*

Gee! And does it last long?

PIPPY: About half an hour.

DEEDREE: Gee, Pippy! Who told you?

PIPPY: [*pointing in the direction of the Boyles*] Mrs Boyle.

> NOLA BOYLE *has come out onto her back steps. She looks about her and likes what she sees of the morning.*

NOLA: Hello, Pippy. Hello, Deedree.

PIPPY and DEEDREE: [*enthusiastically, in unison*] Hello, Mrs Boyle!

NOLA: [*descending the steps*] Doesn't it smell good, eh? I like to smell a hot day. Early. While it's still coming at you.

> NOLA *sounds hoarse, common, but comforting.* PIPPY *and* DEEDREE *sniff in sympathy. Renewed barking from the distance.*

Ah, there are those blessed dogs again!

DEEDREE: Yes, I seen them at the bus.

PIPPY: The bitch's coming on fast now, Mrs Boyle.

NOLA: [*laughing*] Ah, dear! Poor thing! What can you do? They'll be treading on her, all the typists, and the ladies, as they catch the bus.

> NOLA *exits through the back to the street.*

MAVIS: [*holding her hair*] Bark, bark! What can you do? I didn't sleep one wink, Harry.

HARRY: You seemed to me to be doing pretty good.

> *He kisses her hair.*

MAVIS: Bark, bark! All night. And the sheets … they got me tied up …

GIRLIE: Those dogs, Clive, are a disgrace. Surely the police … surely the RSPCA …

CLIVE: [*reading*] Something is happening in Laos.

GIRLIE: Someone should complain to the Council.

CLIVE: [*reading*] Something is happening in Laos, but you can never make out what …

DEEDREE: Would you like to be a dog, Pippy?

PIPPY: I wouldn't like to be a bitch.

> GIRLIE POGSON *has come out and stood on her back step, just as* NOLA BOYLE *returns from the front gate with bread, milk and paper.*

GIRLIE: How often have I told you, Pippy, that 'lady dog' is the expression people like us use?

PIPPY: But Mrs Boyle says 'bitch' is the professional word.
GIRLIE: Mrs Boyle!

> NOLA *has started to mount her steps.*

NOLA: Yes, dear, it's me again! Always in trouble.
GIRLIE: [*outraged*] Aoffhh!

> GIRLIE *retreats into her kitchen.*

PIPPY: [*humiliated*] Oh, I'm sorry, Mrs Boyle.

> NOLA *seats herself with the morning paper on her kitchen step.*

NOLA: [*tossing out her hair*] Perhaps she don't mean it all.
PIPPY: Oh, but she does. Every bit.
NOLA: [*laughing huskily*] One day, Pippy, you an' me'll have to pull out a couple of those loose palings. Then you can come through, and we'll comfort each other.
MAVIS: [*sighing*] A hot day! When the baby's here, I'll sit around and enjoy things. It'll be nice for me to have the baby …
HARRY: When the baby's here, when the baby's here, I wonder if I'll know what to say …
CLIVE: [*reading*] It all boils down to the credit squeeze. It all boils down to what the Government wants to say …
DEEDREE: What'll we do, Pippy?
PIPPY: Let's go under the house.
DEEDREE: What for?
PIPPY: For something to do.
DEEDREE: Oh?
PIPPY: There's a smell in there beside the chimney that's kind of grooby. As if somebody might have hidden a dead body.

> *She starts to go under.*

DEEDREE: Oh, why do we have to do that, Pippy?
PIPPY: [*sticking out her head*] Arr, come on under! Nobody's going to dig and see. Only pretend.

> DEEDREE *is still hesitant.*

Drippy Dee-dree! Come on! You gotta do something!

> *The children exit under the house.* GIRLIE POGSON *has assumed the posture of reminiscence at* CLIVE*'s elbow.*

GIRLIE: At Rosedale, when I was a girl, nobody used words. It was such a lovely property. The big verandahs, and the willows round the house ... Nobody was in business then, everybody was on the land ...

CLIVE: [*stuffing his mouth, speaking through food*] Yes, we know about Rosedale.

GIRLIE: Girlie Pogson—Twemlow then—married in peach angelskin and cream shantilly ...

CLIVE: Girlie Twemlow played a useful game of tennis. Neat calves standing at the net. Girlie Twemlow had a dimple in her left cheek. But Girlie Pogson closed it up ...

A violin is heard in the other part of the Pogson house, playing something sweet and true, but with a touch that is not exactly brilliant. The piece could be the loure from the Sixth Bach 'Sonata in E Major'.

NOLA: [*glancing through the paper, still seated on the steps*] I'd give anything to see a good picture. In which a man cracks a whip. [*Dreamily*] Nola Boyle—Bevan then—went to the pictures. An old bloke squeezed her knee. She got the shivers. But didn't shift ...

GIRLIE: When you've got the home, when you've got the kids, when you've got the wash on Monday, you forget there was a time for dimples.

CLIVE: When you've been around so long, you forget running up the path from tennis ... willows tickling prickly skin. You forget bumping up against the girl on accidental purpose. You forget you could never be around enough.

GIRLIE: Must remember. Oh, I must remember!

CLIVE: Then ... you forget ...

NOLA: [*laying aside the paper*] She got the shivers in the second reel. But went on waiting for the next move. Whose move? That was always so important. More important than the picture ...

The offstage violin plays a sour note.

CLIVE: [*throwing down his paper*] If there's something I can't stand, it's a squeaky fiddle!

GIRLIE: [*on the defensive*] She plays it lovely, Clive! So she ought to. Studying it at the Con. But before breakfast! A girl can't give up everything, and holidays too, for an old violin. [*Calling*] Judy! Remember your health, dear. 'Specially on a hot day.

> *The violin breaks off.*

NOLA: [*laughing softly, her head against the doorpost*] Funny the way you keep on goin' to the pictures … long after you've seen them all …

> JUDY POGSON *enters the Pogson kitchen. About eighteen. A tearose. Very pretty and sweet. Rather withdrawn and tentative.*

GIRLIE: [*to* JUDY, *without looking at her*] What'll you do when you've played your hands off on that wretched violin?

JUDY: [*lightly, because she must say something*] I'll play, Mother darling, I hope.

GIRLIE: Ttt! Are you hungry?

JUDY: Need you ask?

GIRLIE: No. Only … it's one of the things you go on asking.

> GIRLIE *dishes some food for* JUDY.

CLIVE: What I can't understand is what people think about while they sit there listening to music. Sitting, and sitting, like a lot of bloomin' mushrooms.

JUDY: I'd tell you, Father … if I could.

CLIVE: [*sighing*] Well, it takes all sorts. [*Throwing aside his paper, looking at his watch*] And this won't sell anyone a Holden Special!

> CLIVE *goes off into the front part of the house. Simultaneously* ROY CHILD *enters the Knott kitchen from the front of the house. In his early twenties. Very casually dressed. Very casual. In the course of the play his brashness should disclose a certain sensitivity underneath.*

HARRY: This won't sell the socks that keep the housewives darning.

> MAVIS *laughs too appreciatively.*

MAVIS: [*delighted, indicating her husband*] Listen!

ROY: I seem to have heard!

> HARRY *puts on his coat, buttoning methodically.*

HARRY: Okay, Roy! We got to cultivate our sense of humour. Not everybody is a teacher enjoying the current holidays.

ROY *winces.* NOLA *gets up from the steps, humming.*

NOLA: [*going back through her kitchen, singing softly*] Nola Bevan loved the circus. She loved the men on the trapezes best. [*Pottering, humming*] She never ever saw them fall. [*Suddenly matter of fact*] You don't if your wrists are strong enough.

NOLA *exits to the front part of the house.*

MAVIS: Education. Ah, it's lovely! You ought to be proud, Roy, to be a teacher.

ROY: [*sitting down at the table, where* MAVIS *serves him with breakfast*] This teacher won't be one any longer than he can help it.

MAVIS: If Mum and Dad weren't gone, it'd break their hearts!

HARRY: [*patting* ROY *on the back*] It's the intellectual liver. [*Concentrating on his wife*] Look after yourself, Mave. Everything that Sister tells you, dear. It's the pre-natal care that counts.

HARRY *kisses* MAVIS *tenderly, but carefully.* MAVIS *submits, passive.*

MAVIS: Yes, dear.

HARRY *exits through the front of the house.*

[*Turning to* ROY] I can't understand you, Roy. After all, here's Harry and me making you a comfortable home. I can't understand you clever ones.

ROY: [*cutting savagely at his breakfast*] I pay my way, don't I?

MAVIS: [*unhappily*] It's not that. It's as if you wasn't one of us anymore.

ROY: [*in a sudden outburst*] For God's sake! [*Controlling himself quietly, appealing to her*] Don't go on about it, Mavis. People grow up different. We used to have a lot of fun together playing hoppy. Then I didn't want to anymore.

GIRLIE: [*to* JUDY] I can't understand you, Judy. I can't understand my own child.

JUDY: Sometimes I can't understand myself. There are certain things I've got to do even when I don't want to.

GIRLIE: But a girl can choose.

JUDY: Not always.

MAVIS: [*to* ROY] And whatever will you do if you give up teaching?

ROY: [*desperate*] I shan't cut my throat!

MAVIS: [*exasperated*] After all they spent on your education …

GIRLIE: But a violin, Judy! It's a man and a washing machine that counts.

JUDY: It's none of those.

GIRLIE: Then what …?

MAVIS: [*to* ROY] What'll become of you, I'd like to know, when you've thrown away the advantages?

ROY: [*furtively, with a great effort*] I'll write a book.

MAVIS: A book!

ROY: Not a book, Mavis. The book. The book I've got to write …

MAVIS: For heaven's sake! About what?

ROY: About you, perhaps.

MAVIS: [*scornfully*] Me!

ROY: But I haven't looked into the pores of your skin. Not long enough, anyway.

MAVIS: Sometimes I think my brother will send me round the bend …

GIRLIE: You worry me, Judy. You worry me silly.

JUDY: [*getting up, sighing*] Everything will always worry you, Mum.

GIRLIE: A violin!

JUDY: [*suddenly passionate*] Yes! Yes! A violin! I must! Even though it tortures me!

GIRLIE: [*amazed and a little bit frightened at what she has stirred up*] But you weren't like this. [*Then, turned inward, to herself*] Perhaps if we sat for a while in the sun we could get to know each other again. Plants grow together in the sun.

JUDY: [*her arm drawn momentarily to her mother's neck*] But we're not plants. Or only the human kind.

GIRLIE: [*shaking her off*] And I was never a sloppy mother. My second name was always Practical.

> GIRLIE *starts to potter, fussy, but absent, while* JUDY *begins apathetically to wash the dishes.*

JUDY: Detergent's running out.

GIRLIE: How many times have I told you not to squeeze it more than twice!

ROY: [*slamming his hands down on the table, shouting*] Procrustes! That's what we're up against!

MAVIS: Pro-what? Never heard of it.

ROY: An old Greek. Used to cut his victims' legs off ... or stretch them ... to make them fit the bed. There they were ... [*demonstrating with his hands on the table*] they could have been laid out in a row ... all the same ... all equal ... Normal!

MAVIS: I've never known anybody who wasn't normal. Without they were real dills. [*Shuddering*] Any of those others ... that's something in the papers. All those maniacs that murder you ... in parks ... or even in the home ...

ROY: Do you think the normal don't murder in their own way? They'll knock you dead without even lifting a finger ... without stepping out from the row in which they're bedded ...

MAVIS: That's clever talk. All I want's a happy home.

ROY: All I want is something that can't be shut up in a box. Something that blinds ... but by which I'll see ... or know. Some tune I've heard ... and then forgotten ...

MAVIS: [*dully*] I've got the beds to make. Today I'm glad I've got the beds. I don't know about Pro-what's-his-name. Only that ours are first quality beds.

> MAVIS *goes into the front part of the house, leaving* ROY *seated at the table, stiff-necked.* RON SUDDARDS *enters from the lane. He climbs the steps to the stage, then opens the Pogsons' invisible back gate. He is a decent fellow. About twenty-one. Thick-set. Somewhat slow. He is wearing bicycle clips. He mounts the steps to the Pogson kitchen.* GIRLIE POGSON *has moved to her back door.*

RON: Morning, Mrs Pogson.

GIRLIE: [*absent-mindedly*] Oh. [*Recognising, with mild signs of disapproval*] It's that Mr Suddards, Judy. From the post office.

> GIRLIE *goes back into the kitchen, finally exiting through the back.* JUDY *comes to the kitchen door.*

JUDY: Hello, Ron.

> Her reception is gently cordial without being over-enthusiastic.

RON: Hello, Judy. I got the tickets for another concert.

> ROY CHILD *has come to the back door of the Knott house.*

JUDY: [*vaguely, to* RON] Concert?

RON: Like we said. Seeing as you're free … Thursday …

JUDY: [*embarrassed*] Oh. Yes. Yes!

RON: [*suspiciously*] You hadn't forgot?

JUDY: No. I almost … [*Contrite*] No, Ron, I had! [*Quickly*] But I'll come. Oh, yes, I want to!

RON: If you've made up your mind, then, I'll look up the trains. And buses.

JUDY: Oh, yes, it's settled, Ron. We're going.

ROY: [*joining in*] By train. And bus. And the last, long lap, down the road the Board began but didn't finish.

> RON *and* JUDY *look towards him. He has seated himself on the* Knott *back doorstep.*

Didn't know you were interested in music, Ron.

RON: [*unperturbed*] You can learn, can't you? You can learn anything if you put your mind to it.

ROY: If you're lucky enough to have that sort of mind.

RON: It'll be a sort of relaxation, too. From the post office. It gets you down there … the stamps, and the pensions, and all the telegrams about the relatives who've died …

JUDY: [*laughing, touching his arm*] Oh, Ron, it's not as bad as that!

ROY: Could be, though.

RON: [*looking at* JUDY, *shivering slightly*] No, Judy. I believe it's not as bad as that.

> RON *laughs too, and* JUDY *has to look away.*

[*Reminded*] I'd better be going, then. See you later, Judy … Roy.

JUDY: See you later. And Thursday. It's a date.

> RON *goes off the way he came.* ROY *and* JUDY *watch him go. A momentary pause.*

> [*Without glancing in* ROY's *direction, coming down the steps into the* Pogson *yard*] Why do you look at me, Roy?

ROY: [*descending the steps into the* Knott *yard*] You've got to look at something. And it's only natural to choose what's pleasantest in the landscape.

JUDY: How pleasant you can be at times. And smooth.

> ROY *squeezes through the gap in the separating fence.*

ROY: Am I all that rough at others?

JUDY: [*looking at him, candidly*] Yes!

ROY: [*touching her cheek, very briefly and casually*] We've seen too much of each other. That's the trouble. We've felt each other bumping around in the next box. You've heard my thoughts trying to make sense. I've had to listen to your bloody old Bach.

JUDY: As we'll have to spend the rest of our lives in boxes, we'd better get used to what's in them.

ROY: Who's to say we shan't burst out, in a shower of glorious fireworks?

JUDY: Fireworks are few and far between.

JULIA: [*offstage, a slight coloratura parody*] Oo-hoo-oo!

> JULIA SHEEN *enters from the front garden. She is glorious. Perfectly dressed. Perfectly slim. Long legs, neck. A pencil parasol. Any position she takes will be the artificial pose of the model.*

JUDY: Why, Julia!

ROY: [*appreciatively*] The goddess descends!

JULIA: The goddess is late for her bus, and going over on her heels … [*striking a pose*] but wanted Judy to see … this little number.

JUDY: Another!

JULIA: [*complacently*] The newest.

JUDY: [*standing back, appraising the dress*] It's beautiful, Julia.

ROY: Smashing!

> ROY'*s tone and behaviour suggest he may give more active expression to his enthusiasm.* JULIA *changes position accordingly.*

JULIA: [*ignoring* ROY] But the neckline, Judy? Just a little …?

JUDY: Perfect, Julia. Not half an inch either way.

JULIA: Don't want to share all my secrets.

ROY: Secrets are made for sharing.

JULIA: Not with everyone, they aren't.

ROY: Tell me, Julia, will you ever break?

JULIA: I'm shattered regularly by some.

ROY: Do you hate?

JULIA: Not 'hate'. I'm cold. So you tell me. [*Catching sight of* JUDY] I love … Judy … [*Squeezing* JUDY'*s hand*] Judy's a darling … only a girl could appreciate.

ROY: [*ignoring all else, to* JULIA] When am I going to see you?

JULIA: I've lost my book.

ROY: [*as if about to move in on her again*] One day I'll help you find it.

>   JULIA *moves away.*

JULIA: [*defending herself, stylishly, with the ferrule of her parasol*] One day … I'll have forgotten … how to write the date.

ROY: Sorry I've disarranged your stance.

JULIA: [*arranging herself*] Well, I am a business girl. And have an assignment.

ROY: You'll carry it off in that.

JULIA: Oh, not in this. Today it's bikinis. But you never know what you'll meet in the street. And it doesn't do … a business girl … in a crushed frock.

>   *She turns, and starts to make her way through the back towards the street.*

'Bye, Judy. 'Bye, Roy.

JUDY: 'Bye, Julia.

JULIA: [*calling back to them*] I expect I've missed my bus. But there are always others …

>   JULIA *exits through the back.*

ROY: If she was less brittle, she could be less stunning. But would she be less intolerable?

JUDY: Aren't you prepared to tolerate as it is?

ROY: Don't get me wrong, Judy. I know my Julia. [*Pausing*] How I know her!

JUDY: And it makes no difference?

ROY: Shall I drown the less for knowing I'm drowning? And only a glass rock to cling onto.

JUDY: [*quite calmly, beginning to mount the steps*] I'll leave you to it, then.

ROY: Oh, don't … go! Where are you going?

JUDY: To my poor 'bloody old Bach'.

ROY: Oh, God! On such a day! We should be lying around on some beach. Exposing our bodies to the sun. So good for the soul … if it doesn't dry up. In that case: just lying … our skins touching ever so slightly …

JUDY *returns slowly.*

JUDY: [*not in control of herself*] When you're not driving me one way, you're pulling me in another. It's quite confusing.

ROY: [*taking her hand, stroking her arm*] Allow yourself to be confused.

JUDY: When you're not trying to destroy what I most believe in, I can sense we share the same beliefs. [*Shaking her head slowly, like someone tormented in a dream*] But always destroying … destroying …

ROY: If you carve away, you reach the bone.

JUDY: I should have thought you might have reached it. You won't even allow me my music.

ROY: Judy, I don't feel it's your music!

JUDY: In other words … I'm pretty lousy.

ROY: Oh, who ever heard of a great virtuoso called Judy Pogson?! And who wants to be a humble little fiddle?

JUDY: [*wrenching herself away*] If it's names, then, is Roy Child such a shining label?

ROY: [*half ironic*] Oh, Roy can stand for kings. And a child is pure enough.

JUDY: And cruel. So very often, so very, very cruel!

ROY: [*recovering her hand, genuinely*] I don't mean to be cruel, Judy. Or only half-mean. Half of me knows you're the truest I'll ever find. But the truth is always hardest to accept.

JUDY: [*running up the steps into the house, hiding her tears*] I give up, then!

ROY: It would be so much easier if I could too.

He opens the invisible back gate rather viciously and goes off, down the lane. GIRLIE POGSON *enters her kitchen from the front room. As* JUDY *runs off, they cross.*

GIRLIE: [*looking back after her daughter as the latter disappears into the house behind*] Whatever now? Always tears! Always secrets! When I was a girl, girls were bright. Girls were different.

GIRLIE *goes through the motions of fetching out a broom.* MAVIS KNOTT, *now in her pregnancy uniform, has come into her kitchen and armed herself with an invisible duster.* NOLA BOYLE, *still in chenille, comes out from the front part of her house and prepares to wield a feather duster.*

GIRLIE, MAVIS and NOLA: [*in unison, as they dust or sweep*] Laundry's over, thank God! Laundry's Monday. Tuesday for the Cash-and-Carry ... mucking around the shops ...

GIRLIE: And Woolworths.

NOLA: So cool.

MAVIS: Woolies is lovely.

GIRLIE: Got to be careful, though.

MAVIS: Tuppence off tomato sauce ...

NOLA: ... and sixpence on the Snail Defender.

GIRLIE: Specials are never special enough.

GIRLIE, MAVIS and NOLA: [*sweeping, flicking, rubbing*] Mucking around ... mucking around ... There's the pictures, too, of an afternoon. Warm as velvet on a winter afternoon ...

MAVIS: ... sucking a hot caramel ...

NOLA: ... with somebody on either side.

GIRLIE: They bring the pictures close now ...

NOLA: ... almost into your lap ...

> MAVIS *shakes her duster out of a window, stage right.*

MAVIS: [*sighing*] Oh, it's lovely at the pictures ...

GIRLIE: ... for the fallen arches.

> MAVIS *takes and peels a banana.*

NOLA: Slip the stilettoes off for a while.

GIRLIE: Not that we haven't our husbands' interests at heart ...

MAVIS: [*eating the banana ravenously*] The budget ... [*Through a mouthful*] There's always the budget.

NOLA: You may forget the man, just once in a while, but never the budget ...

> *The three wives have reached their back doors:* MAVIS *eating her banana and relaxing,* GIRLIE *sweeping out the dirt,* NOLA *shaking out her feather duster.* GIRLIE *catches sight of* NOLA *and ignores her.* NOLA *catches sight of* MAVIS *beyond* GIRLIE.

[*Calling, cheerfully*] Hello, Mave! How you feelin', love?

> MAVIS *sighs, looking pathetic.*

Like that, eh?

MAVIS: Can't resist the bananas.

NOLA: Yeah. They say you go for them like one thing when you're preggo.

MAVIS: I'll say! I've just about eaten out the whole of Queensland.

> *She turns and goes off heavily into the invisible part of her house.* GIRLIE *and* NOLA *are left with each other. It is obvious they don't think much of the situation.* NOLA *is about to turn.*

GIRLIE: [*making a start*] Mrs Boyle …

NOLA: Yes, Mrs Pogson?

GIRLIE: I've been meaning to have a word with you.

NOLA: Okay, Mrs Pogson. What's your 'word' this time? I wonder!

GIRLIE: As a matter of fact, Mrs Boyle, it's about words that I want to speak. There are words and words, you know.

NOLA: You're telling me!

GIRLIE: And some of them not very nice for a little girl to hear. It's the dogs I'm trying to refer to.

NOLA: Go on! Dogs is dogs.

GIRLIE: It's the female dogs, Mrs Boyle.

NOLA: [*bursting*] Strike a light! Mrs Pogson, you're gunna take the stuffing out of nature! And what'll you have left? Skin! Dry skin!

GIRLIE: I don't know what you mean.

NOLA: Oh, yes, you do! You're picking on me again. I recognise the symptoms. It sort of gets in your nose, Mrs Pogson, that my bloke's the night-soil man. What odds! The money's good. In fact, it's better. What with the overtime. I wouldn't have thought to mention, if I didn't know it might impress. But we're human, too, Mrs Pogson. We have our worries. A sanitary lady's life is not all roses. [*Very clearly*] So, please don't go for me in future. I can't stick picking!

> MRS POGSON *is all a-flounce. During the foregoing speech, the barking has broken out again, if anything closer to Mildred Street, and* PIPPY *and* DEEDREE *have crawled out from under the Pogson house and are slowly climbing the steps. They are torn between listening to the argument, watching the protagonists, and concentrating on the fresh barking of the dogs.*

GIRLIE: [*making as if to retreat*] Come along in, Pippy. I can find a little job for you.

PIPPY: [*holding back*] Arr, gee! It's always jobs!

ERNIE BOYLE enters from the lane, opening the invisible back gate and coming into his own yard. He is in his forties, but very active. An obviously good-natured, innocent and generous male, who respects and depends on the 'womenfolk'. He is carrying his coat over his shoulder. He is happy to be free.

ERNIE: How are we, eh? Morning, Mrs Pogson.

GIRLIE: [*ignoring him*] And, Deedree, it's time you ran along. Your mother will be wondering.

DEEDREE: No, she won't. Mum told me to make meself scarce for just as long as I liked.

PIPPY: [*desperately*] And the dogs, Mum. I gotta see the dogs! Can't you hear? They must be coming down Mildred Street.

ERNIE mounts the steps of his house to where his wife leans against the doorpost looking somewhat ironic.

ERNIE: There were dogs all right. Every mong in Sarsaparilla.

PIPPY: [*shouting, almost frantic*] And the bitch, Mr Boyle … didn't you see the bitch?

ERNIE: Too right I did! The bitch was leadin' the whole pack.

He has turned so that he faces the auditorium. He puts one arm around his wife, and with the other he assists what might be the messenger's speech from a Greek tragedy.

There she was. A little bit of a blessed thing. 'Er tongue almost hangin' on the ground. Lickin' the dust she was. And gunna get a whole lot drier. 'Er eyes 'uv turned glassy. You can count 'er ribs. You can count the dawgs. The big, scrawny yeller fellers. The mangy reds. The woolly mysteries. That poor bitch soon won't be fit for much else but stuffin', and standin' on a bloomin' varnished board …

GIRLIE: [*to PIPPY, piercingly*] Joy-leen!

PIPPY hangs her head and goes inside. DEEDREE thinks better of it and slinks off through the front garden. GIRLIE follows PIPPY, slams the invisible door and they both pass through the kitchen out into the house. NOLA laughs joyously. She and ERNIE move slowly into their kitchen.

NOLA: I wouldn't be that bitch, not if you gave me all the money in the bank. Or perhaps I might then!

ERNIE: Then it wouldn't be love. Love is free.

    ERNIE *kisses* NOLA, *rather hungrily, on the mouth. He looks at her.*

NOLA: Oh, love! Love is all right. But d'you suppose a dog like that likes it, Ernie, with a whole pack?

ERNIE: [*sighing, seriously*] 'Oo knows what 'oo likes?

    NOLA *withdraws abruptly from philosophic speculation.*

NOLA: [*almost skittish*] Won't be long with your breakfast, Ern.

ERNIE: [*as he prepares to go into the other part of the house*] Had a few words with old tommy-axe next door?

NOLA: [*very busy*] Words! You said it!

    ERNIE *goes off.*

[*Calling to him*] Dog words! You know, Ernie, I don't think Sarsaparilla was ever so impressed by anything before as they are by this poor little hot bitch. In the streets, and in the homes, they're all talking about it.

    She shakes the pan and mimes various stages of the breakfast routine. She sings. Hums.

[*Calling*] How was the night business, Ern?

ERNIE: [*offstage*] Just the same, Nola. Just the same.

NOLA: [*calling*] Fed up?

ERNIE: [*calling back*] Nao! Money's too good.

    NOLA *goes and stands in what would be the doorway, in profile at the back of the stage, looking.*

NOLA: [*laughing, speaking to him offstage*] Gee, you look funny, Ern, with the water tricklin' down your chest!

    She comes back and sees to the table.

[*Soberly, calling*] Gotta watch the fat, though.

ERNIE: [*calling back*] Eh?

NOLA: [*calling back*] You're fat!

    Slight pause.

They say there's an Eyetalian going to buy that block up the street. [*Thoughtfully*] Some of those Eyetalians … they're all shoulders and no hips …

ERNIE: [*calling*] Saw a bloke I used to know.

NOLA: [*not too pleased*] Oh?

ERNIE: [*calling*] A good mate of mine. Rowley Masson. 'Digger' Masson. We was together in the Western Desert.

NOLA: These mates!

> *Pause.*

[*Calling*] What's he do?

ERNIE: [*calling back*] Think 'e said 'e drives a truck. Somewhere up in the north-west. Or might 'uv been Queensland. I didn't take it in. We had so much to say.

> ERNIE *re-enters. He is in pyjamas now, rubbing his wet head with a towel.*

Mind you, I don't think Rowley ever sticks at anything for long. You'll like 'im, though. I told 'im to look in and see us.

NOLA: Some dirty, no-hope truck driver! I don't see why you're gunna let 'im bludge on us!

ERNIE: [*seating himself firmly at the table*] Thought you enjoyed a bit of company.

NOLA: I like to choose me company.

ERNIE: [*starting to eat furiously*] I'd rather choose it for yer.

NOLA: What do you mean?

ERNIE: [*cutting at the plate savagely*] You didn't never used to go crook on the men.

NOLA: I like … Well, didn't I tell yer in the beginning: there had been Stan? And you weren't all that holy before we married!

ERNIE: [*swinging his head*] Yairs! Yairs! I know! But there was Stan.

> *The following is performed as a kind of double soliloquy.*

[*Thoughtfully*] How can a man ever know, where there was one, there wasn't others …?

NOLA: [*putting her hands behind her hair, in still ecstasy*] Yes. Yes. There were others. You always knew. But what is a woman to do when she wasn't born mean?

ERNIE: What is a man to do when his guts are twisted by his thoughts? And all the flickery pictures that he sees at the back of his eyes?

NOLA: Yes. Yes. The dreadful things. The mad things. The long, velvety moments. You wonder afterwards if any of it happened.

ERNIE: It's different in a man.

NOLA: Yes. Oh, yes. Men are different. That's why we put up with them. Love them, even. Even finish up loving the most different of all.

> ERNIE *is not appeased. But they resume a normal naturalistic exchange.*

> [*Rather innocently*] Ernie, I believe you're jealous about a lot of silly things that happened a long time ago!

ERNIE: [*dully, automatically, tired*] I'm … jealous …

> *He puts his arm around her waist.*

NOLA: Then what got into yer to invite this truck-drivin' number?

ERNIE: He would 'uv give me the shirt off 'is bloody back.

NOLA: Men do that, I suppose. Still … What's 'e look like?

ERNIE: [*drowsily*] Skin and bone.

> *He continues sitting, holding his arms around her waist. He buries his face in her side.*

NOLA: One of those. Probably yarns 'is head off. [*Sighing*] About the blessed Western Desert.

> *All the time she is stroking* ERNIE*'s head.*

ERNIE: [*drowsily*] You'll send me off to sleep, Nola … [*Looking up at her*] What did we say to each other?

NOLA: What did we say, eh? A few of those things we go on forgetting …

> *Both laugh.* ERNIE *gets up. He runs his lips down her neck.*

ERNIE: You been up since early?

NOLA: Pretty early. [*Remembering*] I gotta run up to the Cash-and-Carry.

> *They stand together and he puts his arms around her.*

ERNIE: It's too sleepy a day to run.

NOLA: [*softly, laughing*] It's sleepy all right!

> *They move slowly back.*

ERNIE: [*drowsily, spell-binding*] Hot, eh? The air lays along yer on a day like this.

NOLA: [*tenderly*] Perhaps I'll go later … when it's cooler …

> *They disappear towards the other rooms. She is leaning on him. At the same time* ROY CHILD *appears along the lane. He is looking*

sunburnt. He goes into the Knott yard, but instead of entering the house, leans up against the proscenium arch, stage right, lazily, thoughtfully, observing the houses. The light has changed to suggest that of later afternoon.

ROY: [*meditating*] When summer closes the door on chalk dust, and foxy questions of forty children, the mind should find release. But it doesn't. Nobody who has been boxed is ever quite free. His thoughts home like pigeons, to roost on their familiar perches ... with the boxed thoughts of those he has never really left.

Here I am, then ... smelling of salt, sun, and seaweed capsules popped in the heat of the day. Wearing its glaze of summer, my body is more or less renewed ... while my mind lurks in stuffy corners, filled with Genoa velvet and silky oak veneer. Where the body ignores, the mind reminds ... that the radio hasn't left off playing in empty rooms ... that the TV will continue to dissolve human personality, like gelatine in tepid water.

Of course, We-Who-Know-All-This hate it, and promise ourselves to escape to something better. But wonder if that exists ... and depend on those twin dazzlers, time and motion, to help us believe we are doing and being. Who can resist deceiving himself when the razzle-dazzle's on?

A razzle-dazzle of light is played on the proscenium: the effect of a blind flapping, light flickering through its slats. While the razzle-dazzle is in action, movement is shorter, sharp, stylised, something like the motion of figures in a silent film, though less jerky. Judy Pogson's violin is heard off in the Pogson house, playing something firm, gay, a trifle harsh—the bourrée from the Second Bach 'Sonata in B Minor'. The violin accompanies the following snapshots.

Here they go now. That nice girl Judy Pogson can't give the violin away. She won an Instrumental Section once. At night her dreams breathe music. Its curtain hides whatever she has to discover.

MAVIS KNOTT *has come into her kitchen. She potters about, scraping vegetables in obvious discomfort.*

All the afternoon my sister Mavis will have had the wind. Her time is getting close. This evening she could kill the carrots.

Barking has started again.

And the dogs … The dogs have never really stopped barking in anybody's mind.

> PIPPY *appears in the Pogson kitchen. She has a mission. She runs down the back steps.*

GIRLIE: [*offstage, calling*] Pippy? Where are you off to?

PIPPY: [*pausing, warily*] Nowhere. I'm gunna muck around the street a bit.

GIRLIE: [*calling*] Not now, dear. We'll be having tea very soon.

PIPPY: [*moaning*] Ohhhh!

> *She goes on, however, towards the garden.* DEEDREE *has come in from the street. She whispers into* PIPPY's *ear. They both laugh loud, then run off into the front garden towards the street.*

ROY: Looking for something to do. Looking for something to do. A lot of it is strictly necessary, of course. But above all it is something to do.

> NOLA *enters her kitchen. She is dressed for going out. She touches her hair in the glass, smoothes her lips, makes faces. She has a basket.*

NOLA: [*calling*] Won't be long, Ern. You oughta get yourself a nice cold glass of beer. There's plenty in the fridge. Then we'll have tea.

ROY: Out and in! In and out! Direction is the least of it.

> NOLA *passes down her back steps.* CLIVE POGSON *enters the Pogson block from the lane. He is carrying a parcel.*

CLIVE: [*opening his gate, catching sight of* NOLA] How are we, Mrs Boyle?

NOLA: [*smiling*] Pretty good, thanks. How's yourself?

CLIVE: [*laughing, rather sheepishly*] I'm good too. Yes. All things considered. Dogs and all, eh?

> CLIVE *laughs again, watching* NOLA.

NOLA: [*calmly*] Dogs 'uv gotta be dogs. That's the way I look at it.

CLIVE: [*laughing*] That's one way!

> NOLA *passes along the yard towards the front garden and street as* CLIVE *watches from the Pogson block.*

Provided they don't interrupt your sleep.

NOLA: You can always go to sleep again.

> NOLA *goes off towards the street.* CLIVE *mops his brow. He runs up the steps into the Pogson kitchen.*

CLIVE: [*calling*] Girl-ie!

> GIRLIE *enters quickly and at once presents her cheek for a routine kiss.*

GIRLIE: [*immediately, as a matter of course*] Don't tell me you forgot the fish!

CLIVE: Who said I forgot the fish?

> *He dumps the parcel in her hands, then exits through the back.*

GIRLIE: [*looking out of the kitchen door, automatically calling*] Pip-py?!

> *She withdraws into the kitchen.* HARRY KNOTT *enters from the garden of the Knott home. He too is carrying a small parcel. He comes forward into the yard.*

HARRY: [*calling from the steps as he mounts*] Hi, Mave? Everything okay? Still in one piece?

MAVIS: Oh, Harry, I had such a day!

HARRY: [*kissing and fussing*] What's up?

MAVIS: Nothing. [*Mastering her wind*] Oh, nothing that you could say. You can't explain to anybody who never had a baby.

HARRY: [*offering her the parcel*] Brought you something good.

MAVIS: [*sentimentally*] Oh, Harry!

HARRY: That's breasts of chicken in a sort of jelly.

MAVIS: Breasts of … [*Repulsion rising*] Oh, I don't think I … Breasts! [*Controlling herself*] Oh, thank you, Harry dear!

> *She kisses him rather nicely.*

It was real sweet of you to think of that.

> HARRY *and* MAVIS *go off into the front part of their house.*

ROY: [*sighing*] The lives of good, kind people seen through doorways! And those we love are always the most exposed …

> GIRLIE POGSON *is scaling fish at the sink.* ERNIE BOYLE *has come into the Boyle kitchen, dressed now, though without his coat. He looks into the fridge. Takes out a bottle of beer. Pours one. Drinks. Belches.*

GIRLIE: [*scaling fish, disgusted*] Once upon a time they used to scale the fish …

ERNIE: [*shivering*] Christ, it's empty in the home just before your tea! Christ, what can you do when you're alone …? What if you was ever left alone …?

Fidgetty, he goes into the front part of the house carrying his bottle and glass.

GIRLIE: [*scaling*] When we were first married, Clive scaled the fish. Under the water, his hands moved so quick. They used to fascinate me. Didn't notice them all this time …

CLIVE *enters.*

CLIVE: What's that you're saying? If you want me to hear, you know, you've got to speak up.

He sits down with the evening paper.

GIRLIE: [*angrily*] I was saying that fish scales—

She spits a scale out of her mouth.

Pfough!

JUDY has put aside the violin. She crosses the kitchen, intent on something.

[*To* JUDY] You might lend me a hand, and lay the table, dear.

JUDY: [*absently*] Yes, Mother.

JUDY exits by the kitchen door.

GIRLIE: [*to* CLIVE] There! You see? For what you count! Now, at Rosedale, when I was a girl, I'd lend a hand by second nature … not only when we were entertaining … which we did frequently, of course … no one in the district kept a better table …

CLIVE: [*continuing to read*] Yes. We know about Rosedale …

As JUDY *descends the steps, the razzle-dazzle is abruptly turned off. She notices* ROY *and stops short. He comes towards her, smiling, squeezing through the gap in the fence. They meet in the Pogson yard.*

ROY: It was a dazzler of a day.

JUDY: [*as he pulls her down beside him on the step*] You smell of salt.

ROY: I'm preserved in it.

> *They sit on the steps, knee to knee, looking into each other.*

You should have come. It would have been company. We could have talked.

JUDY: You would have done the talking.

ROY: *Well, that's so. But another person's silences are good, when they're the right silences.*

JUDY: [*turning aside, cupping her face, elbows on knees, looking straight ahead*] I'd like to glitter. I'd like to know what to say. Brilliant, sometimes cutting things.

ROY: [*stroking her neck*] I doubt you'd ever kill.

JUDY: To feel you might, at least … if you wanted to …

ROY: [*intent on his own thoughts*] You should have come, though. I'd have told you what I'm planning to do in the future.

JUDY: All the afternoon I've been turning out boxes …

ROY: Of what, Judy?

JUDY: Oh, old, useless stuff.

ROY: Such as?

JUDY: Letters and things. Some flowers we found one spring in a gully, and pressed. Remember?

ROY: [*trying to*] Mmmmmm? Noooo.

JUDY: They'd turned brown. They crumbled very easily. [*Practical, louder*] Oh, there was a whole lot I tidied up this afternoon.

ROY: A girl could tidy herself away.

JUDY: It's important to know what she's got.

ROY: I'd burst out of so much neatness. I'll have to burst out soon. Did I tell you … the book I'm going to write …?

JUDY: Which one, Roy?

ROY: … I think I'm about to start. It might even be tonight. Night always suits me best. After that, I'm pushing off. Before, perhaps. I've been saving up towards the passage.

JUDY: Where to, Roy?

ROY: I haven't decided. Somewhere. Out of this.

JUDY: If that's what you want … I ought to feel … glad.

> RON SUDDARDS *enters by way of the lane. He is a mixture of the diffident and the determined.*

RON: Hello, Judy … Roy. I sort of looked in.

ROY: [*brutally, bored by the interruption*] What for?

RON: [*unperturbed*] Why, to pass the time, I suppose. Now that the post office is closed, I've got time on my hands. [*Producing a book*] Oh, and I brought you this, Judy.

JUDY: [*reading the title*] Whatever made you bring me this? *Decline and Fall of the Roman Empire*. Volume One!

ROY: [*tearing his hair in mock despair*] O God of Night Classes …

RON: [*to* JUDY] It's terrific.

JUDY: [*appalled*] But Volume One! What about the other half dozen?

RON: We've got a lifetime, haven't we?

JUDY: [*fingering the book*] A lifetime should be long enough. If you think … I can cope …

RON: You can cope all right!

JUDY: If you think, Ron … I'll try …

> *Bright calls are heard from the direction of the Pogson front gate.*

JULIA: [*offstage, calling*] Oo-hoo! Where is everybody?

> JULIA *enters the backyard as exquisitely uncreased as before.*

Judy, I've come to show my hat.

> *She is followed by* MR ERBAGE, *carrying parcels. He is of the alderman type. Middle fifties. He is both self-conscious and self-satisfied.*

JUDY: [*to* JULIA] But that's … the one … you had.

ROY: [*jumping to his feet, ready to do some stuff*] Never forget Pavlova Rising!

JULIA: [*scornfully*] Oh, this!

> *She almost touches her head.*

This is not it! Mr Erbage is carrying the hat.

> MR ERBAGE *laughs, rather crazily for someone so important and respectable.*

I want you to meet Mr Erbage. A friend. He hopes to become a councillor.

ROY: That should be easy enough … for Mr Erbage.

RON: Live around here, Mr Erbage?

ERBAGE: [*shifting ground under the parcels*] In Amy Street.

ROY: Known each other long?

ERBAGE: [*embarrassed*] Well ... I wouldn't care to say how long. Not to the day!

JULIA: [*helping herself to a hat box*] Poor Douggie's not to be tormented! [*Standing back, examining him*] Don't you think he's rather cute? [*To* JUDY] Judy, darling, let's go up and find a mirror.

> JUDY *and* JULIA *go up the Pogson steps.*

ERBAGE: The young lady can't resist the hats!

RON: Did I understand, Mr Erbage, that Miss Sheen was your fiancée?

ERBAGE: [*laughing, drawing in a fat chin*] Neither was, nor is, Mr ... er ... You might say there are circumstantial obstacles.

ROY: [*savagely*] Here's to trying, anyway!

ERBAGE: [*uproariously*] No young lady ever knew her own mind! I can see you've 'ad experience of that. Eh? [*The parcels jig.*] Eh?

> ROY *and* RON *are at a loss. In the Pogson kitchen,* GIRLIE *has come forward.* CLIVE *no more than greets* JULIA. *The women have gathered at the wall mirror for the hat demonstration. A person appears by way of the back lane. It is* ROWLEY MASSON. *He is a handsome man in his forties. A bit seedy, battered. Good features of the hatchet variety. The Digger type.*

MASSON: [*to the group of men*] Any of you know if a cove name of Boyle lives anywhere around? Ernie Boyle. Sanitary.

> ROY *indicates the Boyle house.*

[*Jerking his head*] Thanks, mate.

> *He opens the invisible gate, goes into the Boyles' backyard.*

Pretty nice set-up. I knew Ernie Boyle in the Western Des.

ROY: [*without interest*] You don't say!

MASSON: Yeah.

> *He looks around. He appears to be investigating in one corner.*

ERBAGE: [*sighing*] Yes, the ladies!

ROY: [*calling to* MASSON, *suspiciously*] That's only the tool shed.

MASSON: Yeah. Just having a squint. [*As it dawns*] 'Ere! You don't think I'd shake anything off Ern? 'E's my mate!

ROY: Ern will just be waiting to have that yarn about the Western Desert.

MASSON: [*looking around*] Yeah. It's that long ... Pretty fair set-up Ernie's got.

> GIRLIE, JUDY *and* JULIA *are grouped around the mirror in the Pogson kitchen.* JULIA *has put on the new hat.*

JULIA: [*preening herself in the glass*] Do you think it's me?

GIRLIE: A bit freakish, isn't it?

JULIA: I'd hoped it was amusing!

GIRLIE: I can't say I like people to have a laugh at my expense.

JUDY: [*putting an arm around* GIRLIE] Mother can't bear to look conspicuous.

GIRLIE: [*scornfully, warding* JUDY *off*] Pffh! I was never out of fashion. But what I mean to say is: I like a hat to look different, so long as it's what the others are wearing.

> JULIA *takes off the hat, and they put it back in its box during the following.*

RON: ... your policy as councillor, Mr Erbage?

ERBAGE: Policy?

ROY: Will you have the public interest at heart?

ERBAGE: Here, what do you mean to signify? I'm standing for councillor, aren't I?

ROY: Exactly.

> MASSON *has come across and is leaning on the fence, listening.*

ERBAGE: And that's a position of trust, isn't it? That only a public-spirited man would undertake to fill? The public interest! Many a councillor has half killed 'imself in the public interest. And nothing to show for it.

ROY: Except the Green Belt.

ERBAGE: [*nodding, very solemn*] The Green Belt is a problem no councillor can afford to ignore.

> MASSON *guffaws.* JUDY *and* JULIA *converge on the kitchen door, about to come down.*

JULIA: [*to* JUDY] Long engagements allow a girl to sort out her ideas.

JUDY: Has he given you a ring, Julia?

JULIA: We're choosing the ring ... yes, if not tomorrow, early next week.

JUDY: Anyway, what's in a ring?

JULIA: Oh, quite a lot, dear, quite a lot. And Doug is so generous …

JUDY *and* JULIA *come down the steps.*

MASSON: [*leaning on the palings, observing*] They got the dinkum oil in Mildred Street!

Everyone else is otherwise preoccupied. JUDY *hands back the hat box to* JULIA *who attaches it to* ERBAGE.

JUDY: Thanks, Julia. The hat's really fab.

JULIA: [*looking at her watch*] Now we must fly. He's taking me out to dinner. Doug adores to dance.

She strikes a fleeting pose.

ERBAGE: [*laughing madly*] It puts you on your metal!

ROY: [*to* JULIA, *with a passion disguised as irony*] I left my flashbulb behind! Seriously, though, I'd like to make a date … any time you say the word …

JULIA: [*eyes just glancing, lightly*] Seriousness was never your line! [*To* ERBAGE] Come on, Doug. The night won't wait for us!

MASSON: [*eyes glued to* JULIA] Waddaya know, eh?

JULIA *and* ERBAGE *go out through the back to the street.*

ROY: I could rip every stitch off that girl, and make her eat the dust!

MASSON: [*leaning on the fence*] I could do something about 'er meself.

ROY: She's all show. [*Desperately*] But what a show!

JUDY: [*mastering her disgust and anguish, to* RON] It was kind of you to bring the book, Ron.

RON: [*awkwardly*] Ah, well!

JUDY: You are kind.

RON: [*bitterly, for him*] That's what people say.

MASSON: [*to* ROY] That little sheila might come round if you treated 'er rough, Jack. With some women you gotta be unkind, so as they can act kind.

ROY: [*irritated*] Does it always take you so long to get anywhere?

MASSON: [*laughing, rolling a cigarette*] I like to take me time. Look around. Have a yarn. There's time enough for everything.

PIPPY *has come into the Pogson kitchen from the front part of the house. She catches sight of what her mother is preparing.*

PIPPY: [*to* GIRLIE] Arr, it's not old fish!

GIRLIE: There's what is good for little girls.

PIPPY: But not old fish! It sticks in my throat!

GIRLIE: [*grimly*] There's too much sticks in your throat, my girl. One day there'll be nothing more to do about it ...

> PIPPY *runs out the back door.*

PIPPY: But old fish! It stinks!

ROY: [*squeezing between the palings into the Knotts' yard*] You've said it, Pippy. Shall we push off somewhere, the two of us, somewhere into the world?

PIPPY: No. You're silly. Everybody's silly.

> *The dogs have begun to bark again.*

[*Dreamily*] All I want is to be left alone. To watch things.

ROY: That's a disease of mine. But it doesn't get you anywhere.

> *He goes into the Knott house, passes through the kitchen and exits.*

PIPPY: [*rocking on the back steps*] I don't wanta go anywhere. I just wanta muck around.

RON: [*to* JUDY] Ah, well. Better be making tracks. They'll be waiting to give me my tea.

JUDY: [*with an effort, to show interest*] Ron, it's terrible of me ... I don't know ... I never thought to ask ... do you live with your family?

RON: No. They're back at Mullumbimby. I answered an ad in the *Advertiser*. I got a room, with use of conveniences, and one meal.

JUDY: [*choking*] How very, very ... sad!

RON: Oh, it's not too bad. When they go to the pictures they let me use the lounge. I study then.

JUDY: What do you study, Ron?

RON: Nothing special.

JUDY: Haven't you any ambitions?

RON: Why, to live, I suppose. Yes, I study to live.

JUDY: [*at breaking point*] You're right, I expect.

> *She runs up the steps of her house.*

I'm sure you're right. You know!

> JUDY *runs through the kitchen and offstage, holding her handkerchief to her mouth.*

GIRLIE: [*to* CLIVE, *significantly*] There!

CLIVE: [*rustling his paper*] It looks like Dainty Bess is going to win the Handicap …

RON: [*distressed, to* PIPPY] Is your sister sick?

PIPPY: No. Soft.

RON: I thought perhaps she was taken queer.

PIPPY: [*practically*] I wouldn't worry.

RON: Perhaps I hurt her … Will you tell her something?

PIPPY: What?

RON: Tell her … Well … I suppose it's something you can't tell.

> RON *exits quickly through the back.* MASSON *has seated himself meanwhile on the Boyles' steps.*

MASSON: [*roaring his head off*] Things are going on round here!

PIPPY: Are they?

MASSON: I'll say!

> PIPPY *has come down and is kicking the ground in the yard.*

What's your name, kid?

PIPPY: By rights I'm not supposed to talk to men.

MASSON: Yeah. But 'oo ever stayed formal?

PIPPY: [*after a pause*] Are you a relative?

MASSON: No, I'm a mate of Ernie's. I just come.

PIPPY: I thought perhaps you was a relative, that's why you weren't going in. I thought perhaps you knew all there was to know.

MASSON: No. I don't know nothun yet.

> HARRY *and* MAVIS *have come into their kitchen during the foregoing scene and have sat down to their tea.*

MAVIS: [*calling*] Aren't you coming to eat your tea, Roy? There's a real tasty braise …

> *No reply from* ROY.

MASSON: [*to* PIPPY] No. I used to know old Ernie. Like me own hand. Never knew 'is missus, though.

PIPPY: My mother can't stick Mrs Boyle. But Dad says she's generous.

MASSON: What do you make of her, yourself?

> PIPPY *wrinkles up her face, thinking.*

PIPPY: [*slowly*] Mmmmmm! She's good. She smells good. If Mum wouldn't go crook, Mrs Boyle would let me spend all my time mucking around in her place. She kissed me once. It was lovely.

MASSON: [*stroking the stubble on his chin*] Sounds a pretty good sort to me.

MAVIS KNOTT *is doing dainty things with her fork.*

MAVIS: Gee, these breasts are beaut, Harry! [*More formally*] They're really bee-yutiful!

PIPPY: [*to* MASSON] She knows about the dogs, too.

MASSON: What dogs?

PIPPY: Don't tell me you don't know about the dogs! The bitch we got in season?

MASSON: Oh? I seen some schemozzle up the street …

The light is fading. ERNIE *has come into the Boyle kitchen with his empty glass and bottle. He switches on the light.*

PIPPY: [*to* MASSON] Well, Mrs Boyle knows all about the dogs. What their habits are, and all.

MASSON: I better ask 'er.

GIRLIE: [*calling from her kitchen door*] Pippy! Whether you like or not, the tea is ready.

PIPPY: [*running towards the front garden*] All right!

GIRLIE: You'll get shut up in your room, my girl.

PIPPY: All right! I'm gunna have one more look before I get shut up …

PIPPY *exits towards the street.*

GIRLIE: [*retreating into the kitchen, calling*] Judy! Tea!

JUDY: [*offstage, calling, stifled*] I'm not hungry.

GIRLIE: [*plaintively, to* CLIVE] There, you see! In homes where the father leaves it all to the mother …

CLIVE: [*folding his paper preparatory to eating*] The Lottery's gone to a bachelor. In Glebe. What does a bachelor want with a prize?

ERNIE *has come forward to his back steps to investigate the stranger. The barking up the street has swelled momentarily.*

ERNIE: [*at the door*] 'Ere, wotcher … 'Oo the … Well, waddaya know! If it ain't old Rowley Masson!

He becomes explosive with surprise and pleasure.

MASSON: [*laughing, rising, pleased, but without the demonstrative pleasure of the other*] Yairs! It's me all right!

ERNIE: [*throwing his arm around his friend, drawing him into the kitchen*] Digger! Old Dig! Thought you'd surprise me, eh?

MASSON: Told me to show up, didn't yer?

ERNIE: [*more soberly*] Yes.

> *He seems to be remembering something.*

MASSON: So I showed.

> ERNIE *gives in to his pleasure and warms to his duties.*

ERNIE: Well, come on in, Rowley. See where we 'ang out.

> MASSON *looks perfunctorily around the kitchen.*

MASSON: [*rather flatly*] Seems all right, Ernie.

ERNIE: [*laughing softly*] Yes.

> *He goes suddenly and shyly, and touches an invisible object.*

That's the Mixmaster. Got everythink now.

MASSON: You got everything.

ERNIE: Oh, we're livin' it up! [*Remembering*] 'Ere!

> *He fetches glasses and a bottle.*

This'll wash the dust down yer gullet.

> *They drink. There is a slight pause, awkwardness.*

MASSON: Somehow I never thought of you in a set-up like this, Ern.

ERNIE: Well, the wife, you know … You gotta make a place decent for the missus.

MASSON: Oh, yes. The missus …

ERNIE: Ever get tied up, Dig?

MASSON: Yairs.

> MASSON *sits tossing his foot.* ERNIE *decides not to continue investigations.*

ERNIE: [*brighter*] You'll like Nola, Rowley. She'll be in soon.

> *He looks at his watch nervously.*

Gone out to do a bit of shopping. Nola's got a sense of humour. She's all right. Not that she don't have 'er off moments. Every woman has 'er off moments. Eh?

But MASSON *is lost in thought.*

MASSON: [*sitting forward, intent, glass between his hands*] Remember those bloody foxholes in the old Des? Remember 'ow we lay there waitin'? An' the snipers up on the bloody escarpment? We used to lie and talk about what we was goin' ter eat. An' the sheilas we was goin' ter do. An' the sky, Ern. I never seen such an open sky. As we layed there talkin' into each other's ears. Blokes were close to each other then. An' you'd wake up with your hair full of dew and spiders ...

There is a silence.

[*Looking straight at* ERNIE] I reckon you forgot all that. You got sold on the bloody Mixmasters.

ERNIE: [*unhappily*] Nao! I didn't forget none of that. But 'oo wants to go on harpin'? I've 'ad a crook back ever since. Lyin' in bloody fox'oles in the dew!

MASSON: [*still entranced*] Remember I once said: 'Bet there's a lot of the blokes'll remember this, and wish they could get back. Even when the dust blows.' What was it they called it? The bloody campseen!

ERNIE: [*determined*] Look 'ere, Dig, there's a lot of that I'll always remember. [*Nudging with a gentle, grudging affection*] I reckon I was never closer to nobody, before or since, as I waited for the Jerries to blow me bloody 'ead off. [*Shouting*] But I'm 'appy now!

Outside NOLA BOYLE *is returning in the fading light. She comes in from the front garden. Her shopping basket appears to be full.*

GIRLIE: [*looking out her back door, frowning*] That child! If it isn't one thing ...

Catching sight of NOLA, *she frowns harder.*

[*Calling once, for the sake of her principles*] Joy-leen!

GIRLIE *withdraws into the kitchen where she and* CLIVE *continue with their tea. The Knotts have finished. They come out down the back steps.* HARRY *has his arm around* MAVIS. MAVIS *waves and smiles at* NOLA. *The Knotts come out of their back gate and disappear down the lane, strolling.*

MASSON: [*getting up, defensively*] So am I! I don't say I'm not 'appy. Only that 'appiness can make a coot of a man.

ERNIE: You wait! Nola's gunna talk you right side out!

MASSON: [*mumbling*] I dunno about Nola. I gotta go outside, Ern.

NOLA *comes on, dawdling, pulling a weed, examining a flower.*

ERNIE: [*to* MASSON] 'Ere, you don't 'ave to go outside, not in my place. I'm not emptyin' the cans for nothun. We're a septic area 'ere.

He leads MASSON *into the front part of the house.* NOLA *mounts the steps and enters her kitchen. She stands staring at Masson's hat on the table.* ERNIE *re-enters.*

NOLA: [*looking at the hat*] Whose is that?

ERNIE: That's Digger's. Rowley Masson's.

NOLA: He didn't waste any time, did he?

ERNIE *goes through a violent pantomime to indicate* MASSON *is where he is, and might overhear.*

ERNIE: [*whispering*] We gotta show we're pleased to see 'im, Nola … tell 'im 'e'd better doss down with us for a bit. Digger seems sort of mixed up.

NOLA: Everyone's sort of mixed up nowadays. There's no craze like crazy, as far as I can see.

She goes about emptying her apparently heavy basket. ERNIE *is in agony lest their conversation should be overheard.*

Where's he going to doss down, anyway?

ERNIE: [*indicating the sofa*] What's wrong with this?

NOLA: I'd say the springs.

ERNIE: Arr, look, Digger won't mind a spring or two. 'E's been talkin' fox'oles.

NOLA: [*pausing*] Foxholes?

ERNIE: Where we used to lay up in the desert. Give ourselves a bit of cover, like.

NOLA: So the old Western Desert's begun already!

MASSON *re-enters from the back. He has plastered his hair down with water.* NOLA *would like not to look at him, but does, if casually.*

ERNIE: Nola, I'd like you to meet my old mate, Rowley Masson.

MASSON *comes forward. He is once more confident, in fact cocky.*

MASSON: They call me 'Digger', Nola.

NOLA: [*coolly*] Pleased to meet you, Mr Masson. Or any other of my hubby's old friends.

She goes ahead disposing of the articles from her basket. ERNIE *is unhappy.*

ERNIE: [*finally*] Nola and me's been talkin' it over, Rowley. We reckon you'd better put in a few days here with us. Nola's gunna fix up this 'ere lounge. We hope you'll be comfortable.

MASSON: I'll be comfortable. But expect we'll be yarnin', Ernie, half the night.

ERNIE: [*looking in horror at his watch*] Not most nights we won't! I've got me run, Digger. I told you I was on the sanitary. I've gotta make meself scarce. Late already. We're short of personnel. The night-soil's not everybody's cuppa tea.

NOLA: [*in despair*] But you haven't had a bite to eat, Ern!

ERNIE: [*all action*] Sling us something in a paper bag. [*Reaching for his coat*] A couple of savs ... and a hunk of bread ...

NOLA: [*hurrying*] Oh, dear! [*Pausing, over her shoulder*] Beer?

ERNIE: [*putting on his coat*] Yes. I can down a bottle later on.

MASSON *has produced a packet of cigarettes.*

MASSON: [*offering*] Light one for the road. Ern.

ERNIE: [*helping himself*] Thought you rolled yer own.

MASSON: [*shamelessly*] So I do. I keep these for when I want to do a special favour.

As NOLA *thrusts the snack at* ERNIE, *and the latter grabs,* MASSON *seems to come between them, and he and* NOLA *almost collide.* NOLA *barely disguises her disgust.*

ERNIE: [*running down the steps, calling*] See yez some more! The springs on that lounge aren't too good. But they'll hold ...

MASSON: [*laughing, calling back*] Okay, Ern! We done worse in our time ...

ERNIE *goes off by way of the lane. A silence falls in the kitchen. Then* NOLA *begins to hum.* MASSON *sits—statuesque.* GIRLIE *has come to her back door.*

GIRLIE: [*looking out, to* CLIVE] Mr Boyle is going on the job. Did you know a gentleman came? She'll have to give him tea. She's not too pleased either. And I heard, Clive, because certain people talk so loud—the visitor's staying the night!

CLIVE: What of it?

GIRLIE: But staying the night! Of course I'm not saying any more. I mind my own business.

CLIVE: [*getting up*] Glad to hear it, Girlie. [*Easing his sciatica*] Ooh! I'm going in to twiddle the TV.

GIRLIE: [*putting an additional shine on some articles of crockery*] There was something lovely this afternoon. Some lady telling us how to make rissoles out of practically nothing.

> CLIVE *exits to the back.*

[*To herself*] But staying the night …

> GIRLIE *follows* CLIVE *off.*

NOLA: [*to* MASSON] Suppose I better get you some tea.

MASSON: I don't wanta put anybody out.

NOLA: There's ham. But some people don't like ham.

MASSON: [*with a sudden sincerity*] I'll like anything you give me.

> NOLA *lowers her eyes and moves about. A pantomime of laying a plate on the table.*

NOLA: And a termarter. [*Gentler*] It got bruised.

MASSON: [*laughing*] That'll make it softer.

NOLA: [*indicating his place at the table*] Go on.

> MASSON *sits down, but does not begin.*

MASSON: Aren't you keeping me company, Nola?

NOLA: No. Haven't any appetite.

> *Silence. She pours tea.* MASSON *starts to eat, but produces a packet of cigarettes.*

MASSON: Cigarette?

> NOLA *hesitates, but accepts.*

NOLA: Thanks.

> *As he lights it, she averts her eyes. She could be fascinated by his hands.*

[*Suddenly, jerkily, blowing out smoke*] You're not doing me a favour, mind.

MASSON: [*sitting down again at the table*] What you got against me?

NOLA: [*mysteriously*] Nothing. I ain't got nothing, I suppose. But … all these men!

She throws back her head, laughing uproariously.

Mates!

MASSON: [*cutting his meat*] Don't seem to have much of an opinion of we men.

NOLA: [*contemptuously*] I know men!

NOLA exits through the back. MASSON does not realise at first.

MASSON: [*eating and speaking, now with an air of self-conscious refinement*] Of course there's men and men. There's some 'ud stink the roof off. I admit. But there's some as are pleasant … well, pleasant sort of men. I'm not blowin' any trumpet for myself. I'm something, Nola, that you've got to decide about. I—

He looks around, sees that she is not there, swallows, then stuffs his mouth. NOLA re-enters with an armful of bedclothes. She dumps them on the lounge.

[*Eyeing her, swallowing*] Pretty nice 'am.

NOLA: [*unimpressed*] Just ham.

MASSON: Pretty good.

He continues to eat, ravenously now.

NOLA: [*looking at him*] You're not starving!

MASSON: I got an appetite. That's all.

NOLA: There's more if you'd like it. I hate to see even the dog go hungry.

MASSON shakes his head. Pushing back the plate, he sucks his teeth.

MASSON: What's all this with the dogs round 'ere?

NOLA: I wouldn't of thought I'd have to explain the habits of dogs to a man like you. Who's been around. Who's been on leave in Egypt.

MASSON: [*laughing, showing his teeth, throwing up his head, softly*] Egypt!

NOLA: It's her season. That's all. They won't stop pesterin' that poor blessed bitch.

MASSON: Ever kept a dog, Nola?

NOLA: No.

> *She pauses.*

I didn't.

> *Pause.*

Didn't ever have anything against dogs. Just didn't think of having one.

MASSON: I had a dog.

NOLA: [*glowing*] But a cat. You can cuddle a cat. A cat is soft …

MASSON: That dog was my shadder. It could read yer thoughts. Used to lay on me feet in bed.

NOLA: [*making a face*] Good job you didn't have a wife.

MASSON: I did.

NOLA: And did she swaller that dog laying on your feet in bed?

> MASSON *does not answer at first.*

MASSON: She sent it to the vet. While I was away interstate. I didn't see that dog again.

> NOLA *is torn between the directions of sympathy.*

NOLA: Well …

MASSON: I loved that dog.

NOLA: You do get fond of a pet. But …

MASSON: [*turning to her, as if to reveal a great truth*] The dog was honest.

NOLA: I don't hold anything against the dog. But think of all those dusty blankets. Your wife now …

MASSON: My wife was a rotten, dishonest cow.

NOLA: [*brassily, after a pause, taunting*] Are you all that honest, Rowley Masson?

MASSON: I'm rotten in parts too. But in different parts.

> NOLA *laughs throatily. She shakes out her hair. He explores the nape of her neck.*

NOLA: Well, we aren't half having a talk!

MASSON: Passes the time.

NOLA: I'd like to have seen that wife of yours.

MASSON: She went on getting skinnier.

NOLA: And what became of her?

MASSON: There's better things to talk about … I seen 'er last at Sydney Central. Buying a bag of oranges. She got shook on these vitamins they write about in the magazines.

NOLA: You're not a lady's man. I can see that.

MASSON: There's been women would tell you different.

NOLA: That don't mean you're a woman's man.

MASSON: Who can say without they find out?

> *They have both overstepped the mark.* NOLA *begins to make up the lounge.*

NOLA: Funny Ern never spoke about Rowley Masson before.

MASSON: I think I meant a lot to Ernie. We were in some pretty tough spots.

NOLA: That's all very well. But you talk about a person …

MASSON: Ern feels more than 'e ever lets on.

NOLA: You needn't tell me about me own hubby! [*Patting the pillows*] Ern's good. Ern's the best.

MASSON: [*moodily*] I wouldn't be one to contradict.

NOLA: Gave me all this house. All the latest.

MASSON: 'Oo else would?

> NOLA *gulps down her disgust.*

You'll have to show me yer house, Nola. I ain't seen it. Only the bathroom. That's beaut. Everything working.

NOLA: Ernie'll show you the house if you ask him. It's Ernie's house.

> MASSON *is very moody at the table.*

[*Standing back from the lounge*] Well, Mr Rowley Digger Masson, I hope you'll get a good night's rest.

> MASSON *throws himself on the lounge.*

MASSON: I oughta! [*Looking at his watch*] It's early enough to please Mum!

NOLA: I like to go to bed early. Always when I'm on me own. I like to curl up with a couple of nice magazines.

> *She goes out back towards the bedroom.* MASSON *starts to take off his tie. The stage darkens and remains for a moment in total darkness. Then* ROY CHILD *is seen in a spot against the proscenium arch, stage right.*

ROY: They're sleeping now. In the brick boxes. In the brick homes. Their dreams are rubbing on one another. There's nothing like friction, even in a dream. Sometimes they call out … and nobody answers. It's terrible then. But is it worse than when a man forgets the language others speak by daylight? It's most terrible of all not to be able to change love into the currency of words.

I've been sitting alone in the kitchen, writing the book I've got to write. Or have I … got to? Have I anything to say? Of course I have! Otherwise, I would not be I. It's only a question of somebody else cracking the code. And somebody must. There's no code that's never been cracked. But till they find the key there are all those torn-up pages … so many dead intentions. Life in the brick boxes is never so dead as the ghosts of words littering the kitchen floor.

There are times, and places, when night itself is the ghost of what it's meant to be. Here where the owls no longer float, the air won't let their feathers rest. The great trees continue to spread, never quite exorcised. And soon, we can expect the dawn … the least substantial moment of all … here where the peewees have died of Thalrat, and teeth grind in the tumblers at thought of another day …

The light increases. GIRLIE POGSON *and* HARRY KNOTT *enter their respective kitchens simultaneously. Mad but shortened breakfast activities.*

HARRY: [*calling*] A nice egg, Mave. Lightly boiled.

GIRLIE: [*calling*] The bus, Clive! You'll miss the bus!

MASSON *is fast asleep, almost hidden by bedclothes on the Boyles' lounge. Intermittent dogs' barking.*

ROY: Turn the razzle-dazzle on!

Razzle-dazzle on. Movements are speeded up.

They can't spin too fast! Turning in the boxes of the brick homes! Revving up! Revving up!

CLIVE *enters the Pogson kitchen.*

CLIVE: [*rubbing his hands, ritually*] Eggs, eh?

MAVIS *enters her kitchen. She is dishevelled, in dressing-gown, holding her hair, her face, herself.*

HARRY: Arr, Mave, I told you …

MAVIS: [*sitting down dejected at the table*] It's no use, Harry. I don't know any longer where to put meself. It's no longer my life. He won't let me alone.

> HARRY *and* CLIVE *in their respective kitchens go through mad motions of eating.*

ROY: [*lounging away from his position as commentator*] So it's no use. I must put on life, as the others have been putting on their clothes …

> *He goes up the steps as the razzle-dazzle continues.*

CLIVE: [*eating, glancing at his unopened paper*] No time for the paper this morning. No time. No time. Read it in the train. The train …

GIRLIE: As far as I can see, there's never anything in the paper. Unless the Queen goes somewhere in that yacht …

> ROY *enters the Knott kitchen.*

MAVIS: Wherever have you been, Roy?

ROY: Listening to the owls.

MAVIS: I never ever heard an owl here. Not since we built.

ROY: That doesn't mean there aren't any.

> ROY *exits through the back.*

MAVIS: [*holding herself*] Never another baby, Harry. Not after this.

HARRY: [*laughing*] That's what we say.

MAVIS: That's what we say.

> HARRY *grabs his coat.* HARRY *and* CLIVE *kiss their wives simultaneously.*

GIRLIE: [*at a loss, following* CLIVE *to the door*] Now what was it I was trying to remember not to forget?

> GIRLIE *returns to clean up the kitchen.* HARRY *and* CLIVE *run down their steps simultaneously, as* ERNIE BOYLE *enters from the lane.*

HARRY: [*calling over the fence, to* CLIVE] How are we doing, Mr Pogson?

CLIVE: Cutting it pretty fine, Harry.

> *Both exit through their front gardens, as* ERNIE *mounts the steps and enters the kitchen of his house.*

ERNIE: [*calling*] Nol …!

> *Razzle-dazzle stops.* ERNIE *restrains himself on realising* MASSON *is asleep on the lounge.* MASSON *does not stir.* NOLA *enters, yawning, in chenille.*

NOLA: [*stretching*] Ah, dear! How was business, Ern?

ERNIE: [*whispering*] Get on all right? [*Indicating*] With Dig, here.

NOLA: [*looking for lipstick, and finding it*] Oh, we had a yarn.

ERNIE: [*gratified*] You did, eh? What about?

NOLA: [*doing her lips at the mirror*] Mmmm. Oh, about life and things.

ERNIE: Go on!

NOLA: And dogs. And wives.

ERNIE: Does 'e like yer?

NOLA: You should be asking me whether I like him!

ERNIE: Well, you know what I mean.

NOLA: By now, I ought to, Ernie.

ERNIE: I'd like yer to like each other. Because we was such good mates.

NOLA: [*dryly*] I'll try then. I'll try hard.

> *He kisses her carefully on one cheek.*

Run along, dear, and sweeten up before breakfast.

ERNIE: I was hoping I was always sweet.

> ERNIE *exits through the back.*

NOLA: [*preoccupied, but calling after him*] You are! You're lovely!

> MASSON *stirs and wakes.*

MASSON: Must have overslept.

NOLA: [*busy with breakfast preparations*] People wake up at any old time in this house.

> MAVIS *has come out into her yard. So has* GIRLIE *into hers.*

GIRLIE: [*to* MAVIS, *over the fence*] How're you feeling, dear?

MAVIS: Look, I could have been hit all over. It's the kick, kick, kick!

GIRLIE: They say it's always easier if it's mobile.

> GIRLIE *has fetched a watering can and is filling it at a tap.* MASSON *has risen gingerly from the lounge, behind* NOLA's *back. He is in singlet and V-undershorts. He gropes after his pants which are lying on a chair.* NOLA *is humming and singing. She half turns, glances, during her work.*

MASSON: Sorry about this.

NOLA: [*laughing*] Everybody knows what to expect.

> *Pause.*

You're better covered than you look, though.

> *She continues with her work.*

MAVIS: [*to* GIRLIE, *indicating the Boyles '*] They got a visit in there.

GIRLIE: [*holding the can firmly*] So it seems.

MAVIS: A relative perhaps?

GIRLIE: [*swishing her can*] I don't know. And am too discreet to ask.

> MASSON *buttons up his trousers.*

MASSON: [*to* NOLA] I'm gunna make meself scarce today.

NOLA: Why?

MASSON: Don't wanta impose on anybody.

NOLA: That's up to you.

MASSON: Later on this arvo I'm gunna take Ernie out and buy him a good time.

NOLA: Oh, Ernie's got the money to buy anything he wants. If he wants it.

> MAVIS *has squeezed through the gap in the Pogson-Knott fence.*

MAVIS: You know, Mrs Pogson, I get worried at times.

GIRLIE: About what, Mavis?

MAVIS: About myself. And this baby. It's getting on my nerves.

GIRLIE: [*swishing the can*] Pouff! Plenty of people had a baby!

MAVIS: Oh, I know. I know I'm wrong. But I imagine things. Of course, they say everything's only mental.

GIRLIE: Oh, go on, Mavis! You've got the evidence to prove some of it isn't!

> GIRLIE *goes off into a thin shriek.* MASSON *has strolled out onto the Boyle back doorstep.*

MASSON: [*to everyone and no one*] Good air! The exhausts haven't taken over in Sarsaparilla …

> GIRLIE *stops laughing when she sees* MASSON. *She is interested, but embarrassed.*

[*To* GIRLIE] Bit of a gardener.

GIRLIE: [*unwilling*] A garden never leaves you alone.

MASSON: [*coming down the steps, very relaxed, well-built in his singlet*] Old weeds grow like smoke.

GIRLIE: [*dashing the water from her can*] Always water, water! [*Primly*] But I'm almost finished. I've got to be.

> GIRLIE *returns to the tap to re-fill the can.*

MASSON: Done some gardening meself in me day. Carried off a prize for charm dahlias.

GIRLIE: [*almost sentimentally*] I like zinnias.

MASSON: Give me dahlias. Zinnias are dry.

GIRLIE: There's nothing common about zinnias.

> *She finds she cannot turn off the tap.*

[*Wailing*] Ohhh!

MASSON: What's up?

GIRLIE: Tap's … stuck! It's the washer … the thread … or some blessed thing. I asked Mr Pogson … [*Struggling with the tap*] But some … times … you can ask … and ask …

> MAVIS *has retreated through the fence to avoid something which might upset her.*

MAVIS: You'll get your feet soaked, Mrs Pogson.

GIRLIE: [*wrestling with the tap*] What's a person to do? And the rates … Mr Pogson says the rates are something crook …

> MASSON *drags off a couple of loose palings from the Boyle-Pogson fence, then scrambles through.*

MASSON: Fix that for yer! Quick and lively!

> *He turns the tap smartly off.*

[*Laughing*] 'Ow's that for service?

GIRLIE: [*grudgingly*] Some men are born handy … [*Looking at the palings*] But I don't know what Mr Pogson will say about the fence.

MASSON: Makes it more friendly-like.

> PIPPY *enters from the front garden.*

[*To* GIRLIE] Fine, sturdy kiddy you got.

> *He tries to pat* PIPPY *on the head, but she frowns, sticks out her lower lip and recoils.*

GIRLIE: I wouldn't know, Mr ... er ... I see so little of her. Now that you're here, Pippy, you're jolly well coming in to eat your breakfast.

GIRLIE *starts to mount the steps.* ERNIE *has come into the Boyle kitchen, rubbing his wet hair with a towel, dressed in pyjamas.*

NOLA: [*calling from the back door*] Digger! [*Noticing her neighbours*] Your breakfast is ready when you are, Mr Masson, and my hubby's waiting.

GIRLIE *continues on into her kitchen and prepares to get Pippy's breakfast.*

MASSON: [*squeezing through the fence, shouting*] Okay, Nola! Shan't keep anyone waiting when the mungareer's on the table!

He runs up the steps and into the Boyle kitchen.

You wouldn't stop me with a camel steak ...

PIPPY *remains kicking the ground in the Pogson yard.*

MAVIS: [*leaning on the fence*] What's upsetting you, dear?
PIPPY: Nothing.
MAVIS: You're changing, Pippy. Always running around the streets. A real little larrikin.
PIPPY: I've got to run somewhere! [*After a pause*] It's the dogs, Mrs Knott. I had to go and look at the dogs.
MAVIS: [*tossing her head*] The dogs!
PIPPY: She's at her hottest now.

The Boyles are seated with MASSON *at their kitchen table. Eating. Talking in undertone. Laughing. Hearty. Happy.*

MAVIS: [*to* PIPPY] That's no way for a big girl to speak. You're growing up. You're different now.
PIPPY: [*pausing, looking up, almost frightened*] Different? I'm not any different.
MAVIS: Yes, you are. You're a big little girl. Big girls don't talk about things like that.
PIPPY: But if things like that happen?
MAVIS: They notice them, perhaps. But don't talk.
PIPPY: There's too much you don't talk about. You'd pretty soon blow up.

MAVIS *mounts the steps.*

MAVIS: [*sighing*] Well, that's the way it is. [*Sententiously*] Girls've got to learn to be nice. Then they marry some nice man. And have a lot of little babies …

> MAVIS *crosses her kitchen with stolid tread and exits through the back.* PIPPY *is left looking panic-stricken. There is an intermittent barking, punctuated by the snarling of one dog.*

ERNIE: [*standing, one arm around* NOLA, *one around* MASSON] I know this is the sort of thing a man says when 'e's drunk, but 'ere I am, stone cold sober. This is one of the happiest days … 'Ere we are, all three …

NOLA: [*embarrassed*] How you carry on, Ern!

MASSON: Let's 'ave it, Ernie.

ERNIE: … the best of wives … and the best of mates … and a bugger like me …

> NOLA *extricates herself and goes about her work.*

NOLA: You're downright soft at times.

PIPPY: [*alone in the yard*] Why do they always know? I don't believe they know … anything at all … or … do they?

GIRLIE: [*calling*] Pip-py! Come and have your breakfast. Here's your kedgeree.

PIPPY: [*her throat contorting*] Kedger-ee!

> *She turns and drags up the steps towards the unavoidable.*

NOLA: [*grumbling, at the sink*] … sentimental!

MASSON: I don't say no to a dose of sentimental …

ERNIE: … when the organ rises out of the ground …

MASSON: … and the coloured lights are turned on.

NOLA: Pffh! You are the men!

> NOLA *exits through the back.* PIPPY *is stuffing the food down.*

GIRLIE: [*watching*] If you eat like that, you'll swallow a bone, and choke.

PIPPY: It didn't ought to have any bones, not if it was made proper.

GIRLIE: Grammar, dear! Don't they teach you any grammar? That is as good a dish of kedgeree as you're ever likely to sample. At Rosedale, when I was a girl, it was too far for fish. I would have given my hair for a dish of kedgeree.

PIPPY *swallows down a glass of milk.*

PIPPY: [*breathlessly*] Finished!

She runs out through the back door.

[*To herself*] Now I'm free! I got the whole day. Now I can muck around. And watch the ...

Remembering, she changes her tune. She continues down the steps, slowly, disconsolate.

[*Slowly*] No, I can't. Not now.

She reaches the bottom step.

If only school would begin. But it won't. Deedree'll come. But Deedree's backward. Deedree's stupid. I don't know why I put up with Deedree, except we've gone and got used to each other.

PIPPY *exits, dawdling into the front garden. The scene darkens for a moment. In the next picture,* NOLA *is walking in her backyard, in a light of late afternoon. She is dressed in something intended to be summery and gay. It is, in fact, a bit off, without appearing altogether grotesque.* GIRLIE *is ironing in her kitchen.*

NOLA: [*strolling, picking at this and that in the garden, smelling here and there at a flower, soliloquising*] This is the best time of all. Before the men come.

However, she looks at her watch.

Even in summer, at the end of the day, when you feel you could have been spat out, when the hair is stuck to your forehead, it is best, best. A time to loiter. The flowers are lolling. The roses are biggest.

She stoops to smell.

The big, lovely roses, falling with one touch. [*Laughing*] I could eat the roses! Dawdling in the backyard. If there was none of these busybodies around [*glancing at the Pogson home*] —thin, prissy, operated women—I'd take off me clothes, and sit amongst the falling roses. I've never felt the touch of roses on my body. [*Examining her bare arm*] Green in the shade. Green for shade. Splotchy. You can imagine the petals, trickling, trickling, better than water, because solid—

She looks again at her watch, her irritation rising.

But the men don't come! They gotta come! When you expect them. Now, or then, it's the same. They gotta come. The men. Standing in bars, with arms round one another's shoulders, faces running together, to tell a bluer story ... Men are dirty buggers! But they oughta come. They're expected.

> ERNIE *and* MASSON *appear from the lane, arms around one another's shoulders. They are fairly drunk. Apparently very happy. They are singing in unison the tune, though not the regrettable words, of 'Up Your Pipe, King Farouk ... '. They open the gate and squeeze through it abreast, into the yard.*

[*Coldly*] Thought you'd drowned yourself in it.

ERNIE: What can yer do? We just got caught up with some of the boys.

NOLA: Oh, I'm not criticising. It's the steak will criticise. It got itself shrivelled up waiting. A nice piece of topside boot, with black onions ...

> NOLA *mounts the steps, and enters the kitchen, colder than ever.*

ERNIE: [*nudging* MASSON, *but less happy now*] Good old Nola!

> *The men proceed to follow her.*

NOLA: [*talking back at them, enunciating very clearly*] I never criticise. I believe in letting the facts explain themselves.

ERNIE: [*stupidly*] Facks ...

> *All three have entered the kitchen.*

NOLA: [*to* ERNIE] And you'd better throw it down your throat quick and lively, 'cause you've got the run.

ERNIE: [*very quietly, more sober*] Yes, the run!

> ERNIE *and* MASSON *sit at the table.* NOLA *produces two plates from the oven, putting them in front of the men with scorn. They look at them for a moment, but tuck in with simulated enthusiasm.*

MASSON: [*attempting a kind of professional charm, looking at* NOLA, *more sober than* ERNIE] I reckon we done you pretty wrong, Nola.

NOLA: It don't trouble me! A woman might have a whole bunch of kids running in late and acting silly.

MASSON: Never had any kids?

A pause.

NOLA: [*sullenly*] No.

MASSON: You ought 'uv had a few kids, Ern. Five. Or seven. Seven's lucky, ain't it?

ERNIE: Cut it out!

MASSON: Why did you have no kids, Nole?

NOLA: [*grimly, quietly*] We tried. But they wasn't in our line.

MASSON: [*chanting*] All of us tried! But none of us has anythink to show!

ERNIE: Oh, Gawd! Stuff yer mouth with some of this bloody steak, Dig. [*Turning aggressively*] What's wrong with you, Nola? Aren't you gunna join the banquet?

> NOLA *marches and pulls open the fridge very firmly.*

NOLA: No. I'm going to help myself to a drink.

ERNIE: [*in amazement*] What's bitten …? I never ever seen you have a drink … [*Quietly, remembering*] Once, perhaps.

> NOLA *has taken a bottle from the fridge.*

NOLA: [*pouring*] There's a few things left for you to see me do.

> *She downs a good half-glassful.*

And it's not bad. It's not bad! Nothing's bad when you're in the right frame of mind.

ERNIE: [*unhappily*] She's not like this, Digger.

NOLA: Nobody's like what they're supposed to be.

ERNIE: [*getting up*] Oh, Gawd! The run! I'm gunna reach before the night's out.

NOLA: Somebody else's going to reach if you tip the truck into somebody's nice suburb.

> *She laughs, loud and brassy.*

All those cans!

> GIRLIE POGSON, *who has been ironing in her kitchen, slams the window shut and exits through the back.*

MASSON: Look 'ere, Nola, give the poor bugger a go!

> NOLA *does not answer. She starts clearing the table.*

ERNIE: [*sadly*] Well, goodnight. Goodnight … all.

He goes out, down the steps, and exits by the lane as usual.
MASSON *and* NOLA *are silent at first. When* MASSON *speaks he appears to have sobered up a lot.* NOLA *is still flamboyant with rage and unaccustomed drink.*

MASSON: [*playing with what could be a fork left on the table*] It's my fault, you know.

NOLA: There's usually more than one to make a fault.

She begins to sing at the sink, wordlessly, rather tuneless, tremolo, but loud.

MASSON: You're a real tiger.

NOLA: [*defiantly*] I gotta be a tiger!

MASSON: But always were. From the beginning. I can guess that. You was born with stripes on.

NOLA: I wouldn't hurt a fly … if the fly acted decent.

MASSON: Ernie ain't a fly.

NOLA: [*choking*] No kidding!

MASSON: Ernie's just about the most decent bloke alive.

NOLA: You know what Ernie means to me. Do you have to go on about it?

MASSON: I was just tellin' yer.

A silence. NOLA *flings the water off her arms and blows her nose.* MASSON *begins to hum, fluctuating, vibrating. During this silence* PIPPY *is seen coming in from the street. There is a whine, a whimpering howl, and one or two barks from under the Pogson house.* PIPPY *runs to the place near the back steps where she usually crawls under.*

NOLA: [*to* MASSON] You seem to bring out the worst in me.

MASSON: I'd say it don't look too bad.

NOLA: What are you getting at?

MASSON: The way you look at blokes … It's turned me to jelly once or twice.

NOLA *laughs contemptuously.* PIPPY *peers under the family house. There is an isolated bark, then the sound of a dog fight.*

NOLA: [*to* MASSON] My trouble is: I've never really liked men. I only needed them.

MASSON: My trouble is: I never had a woman I liked. But tried often enough.

NOLA: Are you going to get out of Ernie's house tonight?

MASSON: [*getting up, looking at her straight*] No.

> NOLA *exits to the front of the house.*

PIPPY: [*watching activities under the Pogson house*] It happened then. She's all … caught up …

> NOLA *re-enters the kitchen with the pile of bedclothes which she throws on the lounge.*

NOLA: [*looking at* MASSON] It would be better for everyone if you cleared out.

MASSON: It would be better … A lot 'ud always be better …

> *He goes towards her, takes her bare arm, examining it as though it were an inanimate object.*

[*Slowly, remembering aloud*] There was a place near Sidi Haneesh. We drove there once. Pinched a jeep. Me and a bunch of cobbers. There was a sort of oasis in the desert, that the Wogs had left, when the war come their way. There was the mud houses. But deserted then. On the edge of the sea. We took off our clothes, and swam in the sea. I had a slight wound in the groin. The water was that clear, you could see yourself standing in it. From the chest down. Naked.

> *He drops her arm. But she is staring at him and continues, fascinated.*

PIPPY: [*turning her head frantically from side to side, getting up from her knees*] But it's wrong! It's all wrong! I mustn't look anymore. It's wrong …

MASSON: [*looking at* NOLA, *entranced*] We lay in the shade. In our skins. And we ate the fruit we found. Because there was fruit growin' there. Vines.

> *He takes her breasts and begins to fondle them.*

There were juicy, black figs. And yellow melons. I can smell the smell of those melons in the heat. The juice running out of our mouths …

> *He stoops and grinds his mouth on hers.* PIPPY *has run forward to the centre of the Pogson yard.*

PIPPY: [*distraught*] Gee, I wanta talk to somebody. I wanta be with somebody. If Mrs Boyle—

MASSON: [*coming up for breath*] … running … over … ripe …

He and NOLA *look at each other, then embrace with equal passion, as* PIPPY *catches sight of the new gap in the fence, squeezes through and mounts the Boyle steps.*

[*To* NOLA] Well?

NOLA: [*eyes closed*] You are a bastard. I've known from the start. A plain bastard!

She takes him by the little finger, beginning to lead him back into the house.

But what does that make me?

She continues slowly to lead him.

[*Sleep-walking, yet bitter*] I was always this kind of a bitch …

PIPPY *has been standing against the doorpost, watching the end of the foregoing scene. When* NOLA *and* MASSON *disappear, she trails back down the steps and gets through the fence. She bursts into tears in the yard, runs up the steps into the kitchen and through, trying to supress her sobs.*

END OF ACT ONE

ACT TWO

Scene: the same. Time: next morning. Early. MAVIS KNOTT *is sitting alone in her kitchen, in the armchair, wearing her nightdress. She looks exhausted. Her head is heavy. She is fanning her face with her hand. The other kitchens are empty. The pile of bedclothes on the Boyle lounge has not been disarranged. There is a barking, but intermittent, and distant now.* HARRY *enters the Knott kitchen, apparently from the bathroom. He is wearing his usual well-pressed business pants, but a singlet up top. He is lathering his face.*

HARRY: [*anxiously*] Make you a nice cup of tea, Mave?

    MAVIS *slowly shakes her head. Tragic.*

MAVIS: I could float off in all the cups of tea I drunk. I got up twice in the night and made meself a pot of tea. It's the dogs, the dogs! Bark, bark! [*Swaying her head in time*] Under the homes, too. Under your own home.

HARRY: But the dogs have gone now. They ran up Ethel Street, the whole mob, after I chased them from under here.

MAVIS: The dogs have been going for days. But don't. It's up to the authorities …

HARRY: It'll be over soon, Mave. It can't last forever. Nothing can last forever.

MAVIS: [*sitting up, holding herself*] No. You're right. [*Frightened*] Harry, I got a feeling it's going to be today.

    HARRY *puts down his shaving brush rather jerkily.*

HARRY: [*coming to her, kneeling, holding her, trembling*] Are you sure, Mave? What makes you think?

MAVIS: I got a feeling I'm going to be swallowed up by an awful big wave.

HARRY: Yeah? Feelings! But is it what the Sister told you?

MAVIS: I don't know what the Sister told me. Everybody's been tellin' me so much, I don't know anymore what anybody's been tellin'.

HARRY *gets up, determined.*

HARRY: I'm going to run into Pogsons'.

He prepares to go, lather and all.

[*As an after-thought, on the kitchen step*] Have a banana?

MAVIS: [*shaking her head, wan*] No more bananas.

HARRY *runs out, down the steps, through the gap in the fence and up the Pogson steps. Loud knocking.*

HARRY: [*calling*] Mrs Pogson?

After a pause, GIRLIE *enters. She is dressed, but is wearing butterfly clips. Could be without her teeth. Anyway, she averts her face.*

GIRLIE: Whatever is it, Harry? You gave me a fright.

HARRY: It's Mavis.

GIRLIE: [*eagerly*] Is it the pains?

HARRY: I dunno. We don't know. It might be.

GIRLIE: Oh, dear! Poor thing!

HARRY: Could we use the phone? If necessary? Only in an emergency, of course.

GIRLIE: Oh dear, yes! I was never one not to co-operate with any neighbour.

HARRY: Thanks, Mrs Pogson.

GIRLIE: Night or day, Harry, you can use the phone. I wouldn't refuse assistance.

MAVIS *has risen. She is starting to prepare breakfast.*

HARRY: [*to* GIRLIE] I'll be getting back, then.

He is already running down the steps.

GIRLIE: [*at the door, calling after him*] Anything to help a neighbour …

HARRY *does not reply. He squeezes through the fence and returns to his own kitchen.* GIRLIE *starts to prepare breakfast in hers.*

HARRY: [*entering the kitchen*] Here, what you up to? Lay off!

MAVIS: There's your breakfast, isn't there? You'll miss the bus.

HARRY: I'm not going to catch the bus today. I'm gunna stay with my wife.

MAVIS: [*bursting into tears*] Oh, Harry!

> *They clutch at each other.*

HARRY: [*passionately*] Not today!

MAVIS: What'll they say when you don't clock in?

HARRY: Whatever they like to. [*Calmer, softer*] I'll ring them later on. [*Soothing her*] Say it's out of the question. My wife … We're all we've got, Mave!

> *They cling together.*

MAVIS: [*crying, softly*] I used to think you was so awful as a boy.

HARRY: [*stiffening*] Eh?

MAVIS: Such a streak! All those pimples!

HARRY: Lots of boys have pimples before they settle down.

MAVIS: [*sighing*] It's marvellous what you have to go through.

> MAVIS *and* HARRY *go off into the other part of the house. At the same time* CLIVE POGSON *enters the kitchen next door.*

CLIVE: [*looking over* GIRLIE*'s shoulder*] Eggs, eh?

GIRLIE: [*shaking the pan*] Pah! That's what they're sold as. One thing we always had was eggs. Warm from the nest into the pan. And shells! The Rosedale eggs didn't break if you dropped them on the floor.

> *Without paying further attention,* CLIVE *has sat down and opened his paper.*

CLIVE: [*studying the paper*] Something is happening in Laos. But what?

GIRLIE: If you ask me, the hens are fed on chemicals today …

CLIVE: [*reading*] … sixteen men shot in Cuba …

GIRLIE: … and that's what we build the kiddies on.

CLIVE: [*reading*] … revolution in Algeria …

GIRLIE: Poor Mavis! She's for it! I wouldn't mind betting her time is close. It'll be today as near as anything …

> *She puts a plate in front of* CLIVE.

CLIVE: [*grimly, throwing his paper aside*] … and the Congolese have violated twenty-seven Belgian nuns.

GIRLIE: Ah, the women! It never pays to be a woman.

CLIVE: [*grimmer*] If it's any consolation to you, Girlie, they did a Pakistani colonel, too.

GIRLIE *recoils.* CLIVE *starts to eat.*

GIRLIE: Clive, there are certain things that … in the home … are not, well … nice.

She stands twisting the pot holder, almost crying.

When we were girls at Rosedale, we were taught just how far a person may go, in conversation, or … life. We were educated, you might say, to look at things ethically. All the young fellows who visited us at Rosedale were hand-picked country stock …

CLIVE: You've said it!

GIRLIE: [*wound up, so that she does not hear*] Mother wouldn't have tolerated horseplay … or words. With the result that, when it came to choosing partners, Kath and Isa both paired off with decent, steady graziers. I was allowed to marry you, because … because they gave in to me.

CLIVE: [*pushing back his plate*] Girlie, I never told you that I've had Rosedale, and all you girls! All the borer activity in the verandah posts and flooring, to say nothing of the three-legged cedar furniture. I've had my two no-hoper, cow-cocky brothers-in-law, and might have had that bullocky, my father-in-law, as well. But he died, at least, before the mortgages caught up with him, belting hell out of his team, two miles the other side of the Railway Hotel at Mungindribble.

GIRLIE *is punctured.*

GIRLIE: [*tearfully*] Sometimes I think you've changed, Clive … that you don't care for me anymore.

CLIVE: Your trouble, Girlie: you think a honeymoon can be made to last twenty years.

GIRLIE: Sometimes I think it's since my operation.

CLIVE: Your operation! [*Moments of perception*] Perhaps I had an operation, too! Only it wasn't by the knife. A man can't stand up to the cheese grater for twenty years, without he loses a bit of himself.

GIRLIE: [*wiping her eyes*] Nice thoughts for two people to have! Before breakfast's finished, even.

CLIVE: [*easing off*] Yairs. [*Clearing his throat*] Yairs. [*In a more normal, mechanical vein*] You've got February to look forward to.

GIRLIE: [*unnaturally bright, equally mechanical*] The rented cottage on the coast. The same work in a different setting.

CLIVE: You've got your own home. Everything paid off.

GIRLIE: We've got our health. And Medical Benefits in case …

CLIVE: And a life insurance policy besides.

GIRLIE and CLIVE: [*looking at one another, in unison*] What more can anyone expect?

> *Here they return to a more naturalistic delivery.*

GIRLIE: And so much happening. There's always something going on. Clive, do you know what?

CLIVE: No. What?

GIRLIE: [*jerking her head towards the Boyles' side*] Something's going on in there.

CLIVE: How do you know?

GIRLIE: I don't. But smell it. It has a really very nasty smell.

CLIVE: Grease trap?

GIRLIE: [*sucking her teeth, contemptuously*] Tathh! It's the friend! The friend that came. And stayed. Something not at all above board is happening over there.

CLIVE: It's no business of ours.

GIRLIE: It's no bus …! We're the parents, let me remind you, of two young and impressionable girls.

CLIVE: They don't go round expecting to catch every second man with his pants off. Not unless you teach them to.

GIRLIE: Clive, I—!

> GIRLIE *sweeps into a position of protest which promises to become tearful, only* JUDY *enters from the front of the house, forcing her to disguise her feelings.* JUDY *proceeds to get herself tea and toast. She is very detached.*

Clive, I wonder whether you would see that Miss Dickerson at Farmers' Corsets, and fetch my bra that they were doing the alterations on.

CLIVE: [*outraged*] Catch me! Carrying a parcel with a bloomin' brazeer inside!

JUDY: Oh, go on, Dad! Mr Boyle carries flowers.

CLIVE: Mr Boyle is Mr Boyle. He couldn't get any lower if he tried.

GIRLIE: [*sighing, resigned*] Your father is difficult this morning.

PIPPY *comes in from the bedrooms. Her hair is very carefully done. She is carrying a book. She sits down and starts her cereals, spreading her book beside her on the table.*

CLIVE: [*heavily paternal, to* PIPPY] Haven't you got 'good morning' for your old dad?

PIPPY: Hello.

She kisses him casually from where she sits. She starts eating and reading. More stylised delivery from all during the following thought sequence.

GIRLIE: Wonder whether I ordered the three lambs' fry, wonder whether blue is right for Elvie's wedding, whether the shoes, whether the thread, whether the radio licence is due …

JUDY: Now that the music has died in me, I wonder whether the silences will grow any less intense. I wonder whether I shall find a meaning, standing behind the counter, or sitting at the desk.

ROY *enters the Knott kitchen from the bedrooms as* JUDY *begins her piece. He potters about, getting himself coffee and bread, sitting down finally with a book propped in front of him.*

CLIVE: [*looking at his watch*] Time to go. Time to go. At least it's time to bugger off. Get in the train. Burrow in with a lot of men. Smell of papers. Smell of smoke. You can relax along with a lot of blokes. Men, on the whole, ask the questions you expect …

PIPPY: [*reading, to herself, in the same tone as the others who have spoken in this thought sequence*] 'After the death of Galerium, Valeria's ample possessions provoked the avarice, and her personal attractions excited the desires of his successor, Max … [*carefully*] Max-im-im. He had a wife still alive; but divorce was permitted by the Roman law, and the fierce passions of the tyrant demanded an immediate gratification …'

GIRLIE: [*as a matter of course*] Whatever are you up to, Pippy?

PIPPY: [*with cold logic*] Reading.

GIRLIE: Well!

CLIVE: [*tickling the back of* PIPPY*'s neck*] I wouldn't strain yourself, sweetheart. You won't be your father's girl.

CLIVE *takes his hat.* GIRLIE *offers her cheek. He goes down the steps and exits through the front garden.*

GIRLIE: Now there's something I meant to say to your father. To say ... or ask ... What was it? But in the end, of course, you never do say to people half the things you mean to. Pippy, the sausages are keeping warm. Judy, are you happy? I no longer hear you practise on that violin.

JUDY: Yes, Mother, I'm happy. But ...

GIRLIE: I often wonder whether everyone is happy. Everybody ought to be. There's nothing to make them un-happy. But the violin, Judy. Why don't you play your piece ... do your scales?

JUDY: I've decided, Mother, I'm not very good. I shan't go back to the Con when term begins.

GIRLIE: [*aghast*] Nonsense! After all we've paid? Your father's going to be ropeable!

DEEDREE *enters from the front garden.*

JUDY: [*to* GIRLIE] I could pay the money back ... when I've made it ... in some job.

GIRLIE: [*sucking her teeth*] First one thing! Then another! You never know what's going on in a person's mind.

JUDY: I expect there's usually rather a muddle. But in mine the muddle no longer exists. [*Standing up, coolly*] Now that I've decided. [*In an uncertain, breaking tone*] I'm quite empty.

GIRLIE: And the violin? But I suppose there'll be a buyer for the violin. Like anything else. There's always someone for everything.

DEEDREE *has climbed the steps and now stands at the door.*

DEEDREE: Morning, Mrs Pogson. Morning, Judy. Morning, Pippy.

They all greet her, though without ceremony, and PIPPY *does not look up from her book.*

What's up, Pippy? I never ever see you now.

PIPPY: [*continuing to read*] Nothing. [*Looking up in annoyance*] Saw me yesterday! Anyway, what's up with you? You look queer.

DEEDREE: I don't feel good. I been drinking ink.

PIPPY: [*contemptuously*] Whatever for?

DEEDREE: Monica Jeffreys dared me to.

PIPPY: [*snorting*] Monica Jeffreys!

DEEDREE: Said it would show up in me veins, like I was one of those dyed flowers.

JUDY *gets up, descends the steps and goes off towards the street. Preoccupied.*

[*To* PIPPY] What you doing?

PIPPY: [*superior*] Studying.

DEEDREE: Ah!

She is too mystified to say more immediately.

[*Tentatively*] Why?

PIPPY: [*looking up*] I'm different now.

GIRLIE: Different I would like to think!

GIRLIE *goes off into the other part of the house.*

DEEDREE: [*to* PIPPY] What's happened to yer?

PIPPY: [*in a wistful trance*] Everything's changed. Everything's different now.

DEEDREE: Aren't you gunna come and find the dogs?

PIPPY: They've gone away.

DEEDREE: But not right away. I seen them early. She's started to bite them when they try it on.

PIPPY: That means it's going to be over soon.

DEEDREE: Well, anyway, aren't we gunna muck around at something?

PIPPY: No.

GIRLIE *re-enters from the back.*

GIRLIE: Pippy, dear, come and help me turn the mattresses. Some mornings they get that heavy.

PIPPY: [*flatly*] Yes, Mum.

GIRLIE: [*looking at her closely for a moment*] There's nothing wrong with you, is there?

PIPPY: No. Why?

GIRLIE: I just wondered.

PIPPY *and* GIRLIE *exit through the back.*

DEEDREE: [*calling, sadly*] 'Bye, Pippy!

PIPPY: [*offstage, calling*] 'Bye!

DEEDREE *turns and goes down the steps.*

DEEDREE: Everyone turns funny at times. I wonder if there's anything wrong with me. I wonder whether I got a smell …

ROY *is no longer reading the book he had started. He has laid his head on a castle of fists, on the kitchen table, and is sorting out his thoughts.*

ROY: [*dreaming*] ... not if I hung around here ... slaving and scratching ... saving up in a hundred years ... Better to cut now. Work my passage ...

DEEDREE *is crossing the Pogson yard, preparatory to going out through the front garden.* JUDY *enters, apparently from the letterbox, with a handful of letters and a parcel from which she is unknotting the string.*

DEEDREE: [*to* JUDY] You got a parcel.

JUDY *continues unwrapping. Preoccupied. Smiling, but to herself.*

JUDY: [*vaguely, noticing* DEEDREE] Oh, yes. Yes, Deedree!

She continues to unwrap.

DEEDREE: [*glumly*] No one ever sends me a parcel ... without I send a coupon ...

DEEDREE *exits to the street.*

ROY: [*in same the position, dreaming*] ... Mauritius, Réunion, St Helena ... Samoa, Pitcairn, Galapagos ... All the world ...!

JUDY, *in the centre of the Pogson yard, finally tears off the wrappings.*

JUDY: [*wryly, tenderly, laughing, but sadly, looking at a book*] Volume Two!

She starts to go up the steps into the Pogson kitchen. ROY *throws aside his book.*

ROY: [*in motion, oppressed by his surroundings*] ... get involved in something! Wars and revolutions are laid on in each hemisphere for those who want to let their blood! Or someone else's. Perhaps it's necessary to kill a man in order to live ...

He comes out of the kitchen onto the step. JUDY *has been hesitating.*

JUDY: Roy?

She puts the mail down on a step and descends.

ROY: [*absently*] Hello, Judy.

JUDY: Do you think Mavis wants any help?

ROY: [*shrugging*] Oh … Mavis …

JUDY: [*coming through the gap in the fence*] Or anyone?

ROY: Or anyone! The trouble is: when it comes to the point, you've got to help yourself.

He rejoins her in the Knott yard.

JUDY: Roy, I came to tell you I decided to take your advice.

ROY: That's rash! On what?

JUDY: The violin. I've decided to give it away.

ROY: [*sincerely, as if he has forgotten about all advice given*] Oh, but isn't that foolish? To throw away your talent?

JUDY: My little talent!

ROY: I mean, such as it was, of course. [*In nostalgic vein*] You could have played your piece …

JUDY: [*catching the same tone of faintly ironic, yet wistful, nostalgia*] … to entertain the relatives …

ROY: … as they sit on Sunday afternoon …

JUDY: … waiting for the scones to appear …

ROY: … and the fluffy sponge. [*Reverting to naturalistic delivery*] What will you do, Judy, instead?

JUDY: I shall become a tee-er-up of parcels. Or I may even aim higher. A business career. I dare say my touch will learn to adapt itself to the machine, and my shorthand will give up some of its secrets.

ROY: Oh, God! And what about life?

JUDY: That is life. The way I begin to see it, it has a fascinating regularity.

ROY: But it's just from that that we're trying to escape!

JUDY: And then there's marriage. I suppose one can reasonably expect—

ROY: You're touching, Judy!

JUDY: [*wincing*] There are others.

ROY: And will you write to me?

JUDY: Write?

ROY: When I've gone.

JUDY: [*laughing*] Oh yes, when you've gone!

ROY: Because I'm going.

JUDY: When?

ROY: Today … tomorrow … I don't know when. But soon. I'll work my way. I've got to, got to go …

JUDY: But what will you find?

ROY: That is what I must find out.

JUDY: It's difficult to understand the things I don't want to happen.

ROY: With women, perhaps it's different. They're more vegetable than men. Provided the bed's well-dug, they take the shapes that are expected of them.

He looks closely at JUDY.

But you're not all that vegetable, Judy. My pretty Judy! Can you resist coming along?

JUDY: Just like that?

ROY: A stewardess, perhaps. You'd look smashing. So obviously disguised.

JUDY: And in the streets of great cities, I'd need every bit of every possible disguise … as I listened to you learn the language of the diamond women.

ROY: Well, a few phrases, certainly. Everyone should learn to communicate.

JUDY: And what about Julia?

ROY: [*shouting*] Julia!

JUDY: But I thought you were in love with her?

ROY: Julia's hell!

JUDY: And I thought you loved her!

ROY: Oh, I could always burn with Julia. She's pretty cold fire, though. [*Indicating*] Talk of the devil!

> JULIA SHEEN *appears from the lane. She is wearing something very simple. She is changed. Pale. White lips. Hatless. Hair even a bit unkempt. She comes in at the Knotts' gate.*

JULIA: [*looking from* JUDY *to* ROY] I came to see … someone …

JUDY: [*suspiciously*] But what is it, Julia? Are you ill?

JULIA: Not really. Stocktaking.

ROY: No assignments today?

JULIA: None. Or none that I didn't cancel. It's not a job that matters very much. Perhaps that's even why I chose it.

She sits down on the steps.

[*Laughing rather hysterically*] So here I am. Craving for company. Languishing for conversation.

> ROY *and* JUDY *look at her.*

Tell me something. I'm all agog. Who is the sanitary man's wife sleeping with this year? Or is it week?

She laughs again and claps her hands to her face, holding them very stiff and straight.

JUDY: [*compassion rising, going and sitting beside* JULIA] Something's happened! Do tell us!

JULIA: [*taking* JUDY's *hands*] Darling Judy, whose only fault is that she's a human being!

JUDY: Tell us, Julia!

JULIA: Oh, nothing. Nothing that can't be put right.

RON SUDDARDS has come in from the Pogson front garden. He approaches the Pogson steps. Climbs. Finds the book which JUDY *has abandoned there earlier on. On this occasion his dress shows an attempt at the casual.*

Roy is no doubt ruthless enough to be able to devise the quickest way.

JUDY: Of course … It was Roy you came to see. Of course …

She gets up, hiding a renewed unhappiness.

Roy will advise some … thing.

She goes towards the fence. Realising the others are in the next garden, RON *begins to take notice.*

ROY: [*not altogether happy at being left alone with* JULIA] Here, steady on! Three heads are better than two.

JUDY: [*with a trace of cynicism*] When one is off its form?

She gets through the fence.

RON: Hello, Judy.

He comes down to her, still holding the abandoned book.

JUDY: Hello, Ron. Not at the post office?

RON: I'm on holiday.

JUDY: I thought it was still some way off.

RON: I managed to arrange it. Seeing as … so many others … are on holiday now.

ROY: [*with* JULIA] Well, Julia, aren't we telling?

JULIA: That's what I came here for.

RON: [*with* JUDY] I see you got the book.

> RON *and* JUDY *go towards the Pogson steps.*

JUDY: Oh, the book! Yes, I'd forgot … Yes, that was sweet of you, Ron.

RON: I dropped it in early. Then I thought I'd come around … and see …

> RON *and* JUDY *enter the Pogson kitchen.*

JULIA: [*to* ROY] … and obviously must. It's not very difficult to tell. I'm in a spot of trouble.

ROY: Trouble? What sort … of …?

JULIA: Oh, the old-fashioned kind! Quite uncomplicated really. I've known for some time now. It didn't seem to matter. Was even a kind of gesture. Then, one morning, you wake up. Dogs are barking. The sky is ablaze. People are asleep in other rooms. The furniture is so … wooden … It is suddenly terrifying!

ROY: Was it Mr Erbage?

JULIA: It could have been. Or it could have been his double. In my carelessness, I was always careful to choose a man of substance. It's the wives who spoil everything.

ROY: And what do you expect me to do?

JULIA: [*laughing and crying*] I don't … really … know.

> JUDY *and* RON *have sat down at the Pogson's kitchen table.* JUDY *has opened the book, but her mind is obviously not concentrating on it.*

JUDY: [*letting the pages drift*] You're so kind. But I'm afraid I'm not the person you think me to be.

RON: You're the person I know you are.

JUDY: But so superficial. Volume One, Ron … it kills me just to look at it.

JULIA: [*to* ROY, *quieter*] But hoped you might find an answer of some kind.

ROY: [*scratching his head*] To such a very personal question?

JULIA: Because I thought you were fond of me.

ROY: Fond? Yes, fond.

JULIA: Fond is a cool word.

ROY: Because that's what I imagined you wanted.

JULIA: [*jumping up*] Yes! Oh, yes! You are right!

ROY: Can you expect me to be more?

RON: [*to* JUDY] I didn't expect you to read that book. Not exactly.

JUDY: Then why did you lend it to me?

RON: I dunno. It's hard to say. I thought, I suppose, that if you had it, it would help to bring us closer.

ROY: [*to* JULIA] Don't get me wrong. I do genuinely sympathise.

JULIA: [*sighing*] Yes. After your fashion. I suppose you do. After all, we're two of a kind. We've never given ourselves to any extent.

ROY: I should have thought you've had a pretty good try.

JULIA: [*coldly*] I have never given myself. Any more than you have ventured down ... off the fence ... into life.

> JULIA *starts to leave.*

ROY: And what about the child?

JULIA: He won't be the first child who hasn't had to suffer.

> *She goes out the gate the way she came.*

ROY: [*calling*] Julia! If you're going short in any way ...

JULIA: [*brutally*] One thing I'll never do is go short.

> JULIA *exits down the lane.*

RON: [*very awkwardly, to* JUDY] I could bring you as close as it is possible to get. If you'd let me.

JUDY: Oh, Ron, Ron, how do you know what is possible?

RON: Anything is possible if you want it.

> ROY *has entered the Knott kitchen. He turns for a moment, facing the audience.*

ROY: Did Julia hit the nail! She drove it in right up to the head! [*With an expression of amazed horror*] And I'm not even hurt!

> ROY *exits through the back.*

JUDY: [*to* RON] If I could love you ...

RON: [*clenching his fists on the table, very awkward, but determined*] I'll make you, Judy. I'm going to make you ...

> ROWLEY MASSON *enters the Boyle kitchen from the front part of the house, dressed in trousers and shirt. He throws his coat on the back of the lounge.* GIRLIE POGSON *enters from the front of her house, interrupting the scene between* RON *and* JUDY.

GIRLIE: [*to* RON] Oh, Mr Suddards, I didn't recognise you. All dressed up. Or quite un-dressed, you might say. For you.

RON: Getting the smell of post office ink out of me nose. The air hits you when you start to breathe it again.

GIRLIE: Has Judy told you she's leaving the Con? Quite the independent young lady. A business career.

RON: No, she didn't tell me.

GIRLIE: You don't seem at all surprised. Perhaps guessed.

RON: No. I know nothing. I only know that Judy will always decide what is best.

> MRS POGSON *looks at him with some interest but does not comment.* MASSON *has come out onto the Boyle steps. He is ill at ease. Unhappy.*

GIRLIE: [*to* RON] I won't say my girls will grow up unable to make up their minds. That is something they'll have from their mother.

JUDY: [*ashamed*] Oh, dear! Mum!

GIRLIE: Competent! Even little Joyleen can run up a batch of fairy cakes. And Judy … That reminds me, Judy, you promised to cut out the yoke, dear, for the dress I'm going to wear to Elvie's wedding.

> RON *gets up.* GIRLIE *fusses her way off through the back.*

RON: When you're ready to say it, Judy …

JUDY: [*distractedly*] I'm struck dumb!

RON: Give it time. Give it time. You'll find your voice.

JUDY: But shall I be able to learn to speak … all over again?

> JUDY *exits through the back.* RON *comes out and down the Pogson steps.*

RON: [*catching sight of* MASSON] Enjoying your holiday?

MASSON: To tell the truth, I'm wonderin' whether to cut it short.

RON: Not bad news?

MASSON: Nah. Not yet, anyway.

> RON *continues on his way.*

Got the time on yer, mate?

RON: [*looking at his watch*] Twenty to ten. Or must be near enough. I set it yesterday arvo. By the PO clock.

MASSON: [*unhappier*] Late. He's late.

RON: Expecting someone?

MASSON: Ernie Boyle. Should be comin' in from 'is run.

RON: Ah! Overtime perhaps.

> RON *exits through the Pogson front garden.* NOLA *enters the Boyle kitchen. She is looking awful. Chenille, as usual, but this morning she does not look for the lipstick to do her lips. She slops about, getting breakfast.* MASSON *apparently realises she is there. He looks around casually, and discreetly looks away. Starts to whistle: 'Up Your Pipe, King Farouk ...'. Leaves off. Goes down into the yard, mooning around.*

MASSON: I reckon it's time I got going. Down this way you can smell the frost even when there's a heatwave on. Get back north. They're easy-goin' up there.

> PIPPY *comes out of the Pogson house, marching primly, as though on an errand.* MASSON *catches sight of her over the fence.*

[*Calling*] How're you doin', Sis?

> PIPPY *looks at him, ignores him, and continues off through the front garden.*

Christ! Even the kids!

> *He pauses.*

And the dogs ... [*Listening*] I never heard a dog in Sarsaparilla this last half-hour.

> NOLA *calls from the kitchen without coming to the door.*

NOLA: There's breakfast if you want some!

MASSON: [*turning, unenthusiastically*] I suppose a man's gotta keep body and soul together.

> *He goes up the steps.* NOLA *is moving about. She takes no notice of* MASSON. *He sits down. She might be a waitress in a railway refreshment room. It is as if they both agree it should be that way.*

NOLA: [*shoving a plate in front of* MASSON] It's cold this morning.

MASSON: It's not warm.

NOLA: I mean I couldn't be bothered cooking a lot of stuff.

MASSON: You've gotta draw the line somewhere.

NOLA: I got a head.

She helps herself to Aspro which she swallows with the help of water. She coughs open-mouthed. MASSON *begins to eat. Detached.*

[*Coughing huskily*] Like a termarter with it?

NOLA: No, thanks.

MASSON: [*rummaging*] Just as well. I don't think there is any.

He continues to eat, she to sniff and slop as if on her own. She gets herself a cup of something, lights a cigarette, blows smoke out of her nostrils. NOLA *comes and sits at the table, but sideways. Sipping. Tossing the slipper on her toes.* NOLA *looks at her watch, calmly though.* MASSON *appears increasingly unhappy. He pushes his plate back.*

[*Flatly, without malice, and without looking at* MASSON] You didn't like your breakfast much.

MASSON: I didn't say so.

NOLA *blows smoke.*

I got no appetite. [*Rubbing the back of his neck*] I got twinges in me neck.

NOLA: Must of twisted it.

MASSON: Yeah. We're not as young as—

He breaks off with distaste. NOLA *remains expressionless.*

[*After a pause*] Expect you'll be glad to see the end of me.

NOLA *continues to sip, thoughtful.*

NOLA: That's a pretty difficult question.

MASSON: Well, I mean … it won't look so bad … when I'm off the place.

NOLA: [*bitterly*] Nothing can make things look any better than they are.

MASSON *gets up.*

MASSON: [*touching the back of her chair*] Sorry, Nola.

NOLA: I'm not one that's due for pity.

She has turned around and is sitting with her elbows on the table, holding the cup in both hands, drinking in great animal gulps.

MASSON: [*indicating the neat pile of bedclothes on the lounge*] Aren't you gunna muck up these blankets a bit?

NOLA *shakes her head. She continues to brood over her cup.*

There's no point in asking for it.

NOLA: I'm not asking for nothing. You can't hide a pumpkin in a bed, even when you've gone and messed up the blankets.

MASSON: [*distractedly*] But you're gunna make it worse for Ern.

NOLA *turns her face aside.*

NOLA: [*taut, speaking parrot-wise*] The best mate you ever had! [*Quieter*] Don't start that Ern stuff. He's my husband.

MASSON: You acted like it!

NOLA: [*beating the table with her fists*] Yes! Oh, yes! Yes, yes, yes!

She calms down as quickly as she flared up.

[*Passively*] I know how my joints are greased. [*Getting up, groggily*] I am what I am. Just about the dishonestest cow. [*Fingering the pile of bedclothes, thoughtfully*] But don't you think a person can act a bit honest in dishonesty?

MASSON: [*not quite ironically*] If you're goin' in for the finer points …

NOLA *has suddenly bustled into activity, getting another breakfast.*

But I'm not a bloke to start advisin' a woman on moral issues. No more than you're a woman as can take advice.

NOLA *continues with her work.*

NOLA: [*tersely*] Choke yourself, Rowley. Ern's here.

MASSON: [*glancing about, very uncomfortable*] Where?

NOLA: In the lane.

MASSON: How d'you know?

NOLA: I heard 'im. I've not been listening for Ern all these years and not know when he's at the gate.

A listless barking of dogs, ending in a whining and a long howl. ERNIE *comes up to the back gate. He is in his shirt sleeves, carrying his coat as usual, but lacking in his customary buoyancy.* NOLA *works.* MASSON *fidgets.* ERNIE *comes up the steps into the kitchen.*

ERNIE: [*low-pitched, to* MASSON] How are yer?

MASSON: [*rather high*] Okay, Ernie! Okay!

ERNIE *throws down his coat. He stands for a moment staring at the pile of undisturbed bedclothes on the lounge.*

NOLA: [*at the stove, tentatively*] Gunna have your shower, Ern?

ERNIE: Nah.

NOLA: [*without looking up*] Oh! Why?

ERNIE: [*sitting down heavily at the table*] I'm tired. [*Wiping his face with his hand*] Tired.

NOLA: [*very kind and gentle, coming forward with a plate of something*] I warmed up some of the brown stew. [*Coaxing*] Remember how you used to like stew for breakfast?

> ERNIE *looks at it dully.*

[*Very contrite*] You used to say you never liked nothing better.

> ERNIE *takes his knife and fork.*

ERNIE: Sometimes you get sick of things. If they're dished out too often.

NOLA: [*choking*] Well, that's what it is. Stew.

> *She retires to the back of the kitchen.*

It's sometimes hard to think of things. Day after day …

> ERNIE *eats.*

Well, I'm gunna turn out the front of the house. If there's anything you want, Ern …

> NOLA *takes the pile of bedclothes and exits through the back, without looking at either of the men.* ERNIE *continues eating.*

MASSON: [*after a pause*] Reckon I've outstayed my welcome.

ERNIE: I didn't say it.

MASSON: Reckon I'll catch the evenin' train to Brissie.

ERNIE: Pretty hot up there by now.

MASSON: That's right.

> *Pause. He has something he can't quite get off his chest.*

[*At last*] Oh, Christ, Ern!

> ERNIE *messes his stew about, listening very intently.*

I was thinkin' in the night … Remember it was just before Christmas … that jerry that sneaked up on us outside Capewzo? He would 'uv got me. Only you stuck 'im first.

> ERNIE *has stuffed his mouth.*

ERNIE: [*through full mouth, staring ahead*] Yeah.

Pause.

MASSON: Well, see yez some more, Ernie!

ERNIE: [*staring ahead, chewing*] See yer some more.

> MASSON *puts on his coat and crosses towards the door into the yard.*

[*As the knife of realisation twists again*] 'Ere!

> *He jumps up.* MASSON *turns.* ERNIE *socks him one.* MASSON *half falls against the edge of the table. They look at each other just for a moment.* MASSON *gets up and exits the way he arrived.* NOLA *comes in just before this.*

NOLA: Want some more, Ernie?

ERNIE: No. I've had enough. Of everything.

> *He turns.* ERNIE *exits to the front part of the house. He is walking slowly, unsteadily, his shoulders hunched.* NOLA *continues on through the kitchen and down the steps, like a sleepwalker.*

NOLA: The terrible thing about a conscience is it don't stay with you all the time. It walks out, and lets you down. When you're weak.

> *She reaches the bottom of the steps. She twists off a flower.*

I'm weak. [*Tearing the flower, walking and meditating*] There are times when the flesh lies too easy on your bones. When even the air tickles your skin, in the places where it can get at you most. I can't help it if I want to dance at odd moments. Or if somebody else joins in. After all, I'm only half-wanting what I can't help.

> *She throws away the flower she has been tearing, disgusted.*

I would like to be left in peace with what I respect most, and love. Not kill. [*In a panic of shivers*] I don't wanta kill! Thank Gawd, I never ran the knife all that far. Or did I?! [*Holding her head, in agony*] Have I? You do if you keep at it! [*Throwing up her head in a blaze of protest*] Whether you like it or not. [*After a pause, choking, running her hands down her flanks*] It's this blasted body! It's put together wrong. If your hips was to work different ... Or there weren't none of those pulses in your throat. [*Looking up at the Pogson house, bitterly*] I bet some women aren't all that good. They just haven't got the kind of glands it takes to make a person go to the pack.

PIPPY *returns from her errand. Approaching from the front garden, she enters the Pogson yard. Quickly realising* MRS BOYLE *is in hers, she advances cautiously, hoping to make the back steps without becoming involved in conversation.*

[*Looking over the fence, with immense relief*] Is that you, Pippy?

PIPPY: [*embarrassed, cautious, mincing slightly*] Yes.

NOLA: Oh, I'm so glad to see you! I haven't seen you, Pippy, since I don't know when.

PIPPY: It was only yesterday, Mrs Boyle.

NOLA: Was it? Well, a lot has happened. I mean … I've been sort of busy. Had a few problems on me mind …

PIPPY *has continued standing, out of politeness, but remains silent. A look of isolation about her.*

Then you begin to miss the faces you haven't noticed.

PIPPY *is silent.* NOLA *senses something.*

[*In desperation*] You remember once—we said how good it would be if only there was a hole in that fence, so as you could crawl through, and we could comfort each other? Well, there! [*Pointing*] Somebody's made the hole!

PIPPY: Yes. That was Mr Masson.

NOLA: Oh, I don't care who did it!

PIPPY: Dad says Mr Masson is liable. He went real crook.

NOLA: [*sighing*] Ah, we can put it back then. If it'll make anybody feel safe.

Pause.

You'll never cure some people of being afraid.

PIPPY, *after seeming to hesitate, accepts a challenge.*

PIPPY: I'll come through, if you want me to.

NOLA: [*snootily*] I don't want you to do anything your parents wouldn't want.

PIPPY: [*squeezing through*] Oh, them!

She seems to recover something of her old form at the mention of her parents.

I do what I want, you know. I only let them think I don't.

NOLA: [*putting an arm around* PIPPY] That's all right, so long as you don't do too much of it.

> *They stroll a little, describing an arc in the yard before approaching the steps.* PIPPY *walks very stiffly inside the encircling arm.*

[*Encouragingly*] Well now, it's quite like old times.
PIPPY: I dunno.
NOLA: No. You got something. It's not. It's never the same again.

> *Pause, as they mount the steps.*

[*Hopefully*] Aren't you gunna tell me something? What about those blessed dogs you was always talking about?

> PIPPY *is embarrassed. They stand together on the steps.*

PIPPY: I'm not all that interested in dogs anymore.
NOLA: Oh?
PIPPY: Anyhow, they're going away. I think it's going to be over soon.
NOLA: Could be. They was at it long enough.
PIPPY: Anyway, I don't like dogs. Dogs are dirty.
NOLA: [*surprised*] You were such a one for dogs before.
PIPPY: But they're dirty. You didn't ought to take any notice of them when they carry on like that.
NOLA: They're teaching you fast! [*Sadly, nodding her head*] Well, perhaps it's all for the best.

> NOLA *goes on up the steps.* PIPPY *remains halfway up.*

PIPPY: I mean, you can notice, but you mustn't look.
NOLA: [*laughing softly, sadly*] That's the way it is! [*In the doorway*] Aren't you coming in, Pippy?
PIPPY: What … in there?
NOLA: It won't give you leprosy!

> PIPPY *glances over her shoulder at her own home.*

But if your mum and dad are in any way—

> PIPPY *marches up the steps and enters the kitchen behind* NOLA.

[*Delighted, expanding again*] There! [*Fussing around*] I'm gunna give you a treat.
PIPPY: [*doubtfully*] What?
NOLA: [*searching for something*] If I can find it … [*Searching*] I got a box of marshmallers stuck away somewhere.

PIPPY: [*wrinkling her nose, but politely*] Oh.

NOLA: Don't you like marshmallers, Pippy? I've always liked marshmallers. [*Finding them*] There! They're that soft. Scenty, too.

> She offers and PIPPY takes one unenthusiastically.

PIPPY: I like Paddle Pops best.

NOLA: [*stuffing her mouth*] That's all right! But how am I gunna produce Paddle Pops out of me fanny adams for every little casual girl?

PIPPY: [*laughing her head off*] Fanny adams!

NOLA: [*laughing too*] Well?

PIPPY: [*choking*] It's funny.

NOLA: What's true is often funny too. [*Sighing*] Ah, dear!

PIPPY: [*frowning at the marshmallow*] This has got a sort of funny smell.

NOLA: That's the scent. [*Surprised*] Don't you like it?

> PIPPY *wrinkles her nose again. Does not answer. She takes small, careful bites.*

[*Through full mouth*] I think it's lovely.

PIPPY: [*thawing, looking about her*] It's lovely in here.

> She walks around, examining things. Carefully she puts her marshmallow down somewhere.

NOLA: What's so different about it?

PIPPY: [*prowling*] Oh, I dunno. You can be natural in it.

> NOLA *looks glum.*

[*Landing on the sofa*] This lounge!

> She wriggles about on it.

NOLA: [*contemptuously*] That old thing! Springs are gone.

PIPPY: [*trying to bounce*] No, they're not. Not this end. All our furniture's stuffed too full. And Mum won't let us do anything on it.

NOLA: [*quietly*] I hate that old lounge.

> She glances towards the other part of the house, listening.

And you could disturb Mr Boyle. He's trying to get some sleep after the night run.

> PIPPY *remembers something. Cautious again, she starts prowling around.*

PIPPY: [*carefully*] Are you lonely when you're all alone at home at night?

NOLA: [*equally careful*] Other women have the daytime to be lonely in. It amounts to the same thing.

PIPPY: One night I was feeling lonely. I wanted to come in.

NOLA: You ought 'uv.

PIPPY: I did. [*Quickly*] I didn't, I mean! [*Tracing something on the furniture*] I was afraid.

NOLA: [*suspiciously, nostrils dilating*] Are you your mother's daughter?

PIPPY: [*surprised and suspicious in turn*] Me mother's daughter?

NOLA: [*quickly, shrugging it off*] It's a way of speaking.

PIPPY: We got somebody like that at school. Only it's the father.

NOLA: Oh, Gawd! You're your mother's daughter, and your father's, if that's what you wanta know. Only you're not. See?

PIPPY: [*rather dismally*] Mum's all right. She can't help it.

> *Pause.*

I like you, Mrs Boyle.

NOLA: [*going to* PIPPY, *half tearfully*] That's the first blessed thing I've liked hearing today!

> NOLA *puts her arms around* PIPPY, *who submits, but is embarrassed and shy.* NOLA *draws her down onto the sofa.*

[*Dreamily*] The first thing!

PIPPY: [*submitting, but very careful*] I love you. I love the way you smell.

NOLA: Eh?

PIPPY: You smell good.

NOLA: What of?

PIPPY: Of bread.

NOLA: That's harmless enough to please anybody!

PIPPY: And tinned peaches.

NOLA: Well, waddaya know!

PIPPY: Those big yellow ones.

NOLA: [*trying to trap the child's head*] Pippy, don't say any more, dear. You'll spoil it!

> *A short silence, in which their composition remains rather awkward.*

PIPPY: [*tentatively*] About those dogs …

NOLA: [*withdrawing*] We're on to that subject again!

PIPPY: The bitch ... What'll happen to her ... when the dogs can't get any more, and go?

NOLA: [*unhappily*] That's one way of putting it! [*Pausing*] Well, she'll go away and have pups.

PIPPY: Pups!

NOLA: Yes. Don't you like them?

PIPPY: Oh, yes. They're lovely. But do all bitches have pups after ... after it's happened?

NOLA: [*sombrely*] Some bitches are lucky enough to escape. Some of the time. I mean, it's lucky for those street bitches. What'd they do with a lot of pups? Just roaming around. After they're turned out.

PIPPY: Are they?

NOLA: Some of them are. Their owners can't take what's been happening. And it happens again.

PIPPY: What, all over again?

NOLA: Yes. Every six months. That's nature.

She breaks down. PIPPY *is at first surprised, then horrified.*

PIPPY: [*shaking* NOLA, *frightened*] Mrs Boyle! Don't, Mrs Boyle! We're not going to talk about it.

NOLA: [*blowing her nose*] But it happens ... that way ...

ERNIE BOYLE *enters from the back. He is rubbing his head with a towel, dressed in pyjamas.*

[*Realising without turning, repairing the damage*] Aren't you gunna get your sleep, Ern?

ERNIE: Sleep!

He does not look at NOLA. *He struts about, drying his hair.*

Haven't seen you, Pippy.

PIPPY: I've been here.

ERNIE: Must 'uv been keeping yourself dark.

He sits down on the doorstep with his back to the others.

What 'uv you been up to?

Both ERNIE *and* NOLA *are clinging desperately to* PIPPY's *presence.*

NOLA: She's been studyin'.

ERNIE: No kiddin'!

NOLA: She's been reading books.

ERNIE: What about, eh? Science? That's what they all go for now.

PIPPY: No. Emperors and empresses. And murders. *Decline and Fall of the Roman Empire.*

ERNIE: I never read a book like that. I wouldn't know about that.

NOLA: Sounds dry to me. Even with the murders.

PIPPY: [*getting up*] There are the dry bits. But there's the other bits as well.

ERNIE: But emperors and empresses! They wouldn't make sense today. Only on the pictures.

> PIPPY *approaches the back door, wondering how she can get by.*

PIPPY: Oh, they're the same. Everybody's the same. Even dogs are.

> ERNIE *and* NOLA *realise she wants to leave. Their horror grows.*

ERNIE: [*to* PIPPY] You ain't goin', are yer?

PIPPY: Yes.

ERNIE: We like to have yer talk, Pippy … tell us things. An educated girl. And you're gunna walk out …

PIPPY: [*very quietly*] I've said all I've got to say.

NOLA: [*looking at her lap*] That's a pretty good reason.

> PIPPY *squeezes past* ERNIE *on the step. She goes down, gets through the fence and disappears into her own house. All of it she does very smoothly. Her thoughts are for the moment totally disguised. The following short reverie of the Boyles should be spoken as if from an inescapable nightmare.*

ERNIE: When you're left alone together, that's when the trouble begins.

NOLA: You can't cut the silences anyhow.

ERNIE: You're surrounded by bloody furniture.

NOLA: And thoughts.

ERNIE: I remember the Sunday at Manly. We got half boiled by the sun. There was hairs on your wrist I'd never noticed before. The sand tricklin' down the little blonde hairs …

NOLA: I remember 1948. I thought I'd copped it at last. I was carrying you! You. And we tore the cold chicken apart. And we toasted him in real wine, like the social set do. But it was only another false alarm …

Here they resume a naturalistic delivery.

You ought to lie down, Ern. Try to get some sleep.

ERNIE: [*jumping up irritably, ignoring her*] Nao.

NOLA: You'll be dog tired.

ERNIE: I can get bloody-well flogged for all I care.

NOLA: [*avoiding looking at him*] Sit on the front verandah, then. It's nice and cool.

ERNIE: Sit on the front verandah, and watch 'em saying: 'He must be the only one who doesn't know!'

ERNIE *exits to the front of the house, avoiding her. A distinct, sharp moan is heard from offstage in the Knotts' house. At Pogsons'* GIRLIE *comes running out from the front rooms to her back door.* NOLA *gets up and comes, slower, but anxious, to hers.* GIRLIE *and* NOLA *both crane in the direction of Knotts'. Another stifled moan as* HARRY KNOTT *appears in his kitchen, very agitated. He runs down the steps.*

GIRLIE: [*calling*] Is it the pains, Harry?

GIRLIE *starts down her own steps, equally agitated, to meet him.*

HARRY: It's the pains all right! It's begun! We didn't ought of … I was all for … Mrs Pogson, can I use the phone?

HARRY *gets through the fence.*

GIRLIE: [*spinning around*] Oh, dear! Yes!

GIRLIE *gets through the fence into the Knotts'.*

HARRY: [*mounting the Pogson steps*] If she'd only done what Sister told her …

GIRLIE *is all of a dither. After approaching the Knott steps, she thinks better of it.*

GIRLIE: [*undecided*] Oh, dear! Some women don't like … [*Deciding, calling*] Harry, I'd better come and show you. There's a little trick … [*getting back through the fence*] in dialling. [*Running back towards her own steps*] Everybody's phone has something special that you've got to learn …

HARRY *has disappeared into the front of the Pogson house,* GIRLIE *following.* NOLA *has leant against her doorpost, facing away from the Knotts', but not from lack of sympathy.*

NOLA: [*rubbing her head against the doorpost, swaying very slightly*] The pains have got her. It's happening to Mavis Knott. Always a decent, dumb cow. One of the lucky ones. She'll settle down to it like shelling peas. Wonder whether I could have stood that pain. [*Closing her eyes, gritting her teeth*] Tearing me in half. Tearing. But, oh God, what lovely ... lovely ... relief ... [*Opening her eyes, savagely*] Of course I could 'uv stood it! It's nothing to what you bear in your mind ...

HARRY *reappears in the Pogson kitchen, looking rather dazed. He is followed by* GIRLIE, JUDY *and* PIPPY.

GIRLIE: [*assuring him*] If there's anything I can do for Mavis, Harry ... Always oblige a neighbour if I can ...

MAVIS *has meanwhile entered her kitchen, walking very slowly, heavily, holding herself, supported by* ROY. *She is wearing her overcoat. She seats herself carefully in the armchair, waiting in a trance.* ROY *squats beside* MAVIS, *holding her hand.* HARRY *runs back to his own house. The three Pogsons all gather at their back door.*

PIPPY: I'm never gunna have a baby if it hurts like that! Ugh!

JUDY *shushes her.* HARRY *arrives in his own kitchen.*

HARRY: I rung, dear. You oughta wait. They'll fetch a stretcher.

MAVIS *does not answer. She sits supporting her head. Pale.* DEEDREE *enters from the Pogson front garden. She comes on at a skipping pace into the yard.*

PIPPY: [*to* GIRLIE] But doesn't it hurt?

GIRLIE: Pippy, my nerves won't stand any more! [*Glancing, realising* NOLA BOYLE *is at her door*] It's something, Mrs Boyle, that only a woman can understand. Take the husband ... Harry is good ...

NOLA: [*vigorously*] Harry is good!

GIRLIE: But poor fellow ... it's not the same ...

NOLA: It's never the same.

GIRLIE *and* NOLA *seem to have discovered each other, and to have formed an alliance.*

[*Looking at the sky*] And on such a day!

GIRLIE: It's hot all right.

NOLA: And will get hotter.

MAVIS: [*stirring*] I'll be all right. I got a fright. [*To* ROY] Roy, dear, I want to be with Harry a little. I'm silly. That's all. But with Harry ... till the ambulance ...

ROY *pats her. He goes down into the yard. Walks about. Lights a cigarette. Ends up leaning against the proscenium arch.*

GIRLIE: [*to* NOLA] Already at six o'clock I said to Mr Pogson: 'Clive,' I said, 'already I feel I'm going around under the lid of a big copper. Pressing down ... down ...'

NOLA *shakes her head and sucks her teeth in sympathy.* DEEDREE *has approached and mounts the lower steps.*

DEEDREE: What's up, Pippy?

PIPPY: Shut up, silly!

MAVIS: [*to* HARRY] There's something I want you to remember, dear. You must always take the bus. Never get carried away. Taxis'll drain you dry. From Sarsaparilla to Barranugli. Take the bus to the hospital. We'll need every penny now. It's the pennies that count.

HARRY *puts his arms around her, comforting.*

GIRLIE: [*to* NOLA, *indicating* ROY] There's the brother. Blood, maybe. But never so close as a woman. Even the neighbour is closer than a brother.

NOLA *nods her head. The ambulance is heard in the distance, approaching always closer.*

DEEDREE: [*to* PIPPY] Is somebody sick? Has there been an accident?

PIPPY: Get her!

GIRLIE *gives* PIPPY *a push.* JUDY *is unable to remain where she is any longer. She goes down to* ROY. *He holds out his hand to her and draws her into the shadow of the Knotts' yard.*

MAVIS: [*very serious*] There's something I want you to know, Harry.

HARRY: What?

MAVIS: I'm glad I'm not having this baby with anybody else.

HARRY: [*glad, helpless, comforting*] I should hope so, dear!

The ambulance apparently comes to a stop.

MAVIS: For instance, I can't think what it'd be like to have it with Mr Pogson.

HARRY: No. Clive Pogson's a decent enough cove. But not to go having babies with.

Two AMBULANCE MEN *enter from the Knotts' front garden. They have a stretcher.*

GIRLIE: [*excitedly, to* NOLA] The ambulance!

The AMBULANCE MEN *advance.*

FIRST MAN: [*to* ROY] Home of Mr H. Knott?

ROY: That's right. [*Calling*] Harry, the ambulance!

GIRLIE: [*simultaneously, pointing*] In there! I bet she'll be relieved.

NOLA: Yes, poor thing!

The AMBULANCE MEN *ascend.*

DEEDREE: [*to* PIPPY] Is somebody having a baby?

PIPPY: You'll kill me!

The AMBULANCE MEN *enter the Knott kitchen.*

FIRST MAN: Mrs Knott? We'll have you there before you know you've left your own home.

MAVIS: But I'm all right now. I'm not. But you know … it comes and goes. It puts the wind up you at times.

The AMBULANCE MEN *arrange the stretcher.*

HARRY: [*hoarsely*] There you are, dear. Do everything they say.

SECOND MAN: [*asserting himself, jovially*] How are yer for weight, Mrs Knott?

MAVIS: [*drawing back*] Oh, but I don't wanta go on a stretcher! I can leave home on me own feet. If I take it slow.

FIRST MAN: [*a bit dry*] It's up to you.

HARRY: I'd do what they say, dear. After all, we subscribe to it.

MAVIS: [*thoughtfully*] Yes … well … if we've paid for it …

She allows herself to be helped to lie down.

[*Fretfully*] Only I never thought I'd leave me own home on a stretcher. All the neighbours waiting for a body …

GIRLIE: [*craning, to* NOLA] Do you think anything can have gone wrong?

NOLA: They do say those men are very capable.

GIRLIE: Can deliver at a pinch …

MAVIS: [*on the stretcher*] Harry, you'll have to stop the milk.

HARRY: [*going around in circles*] The milk? The milk … Yes, the milk!

GIRLIE: [*frustrated, to* NOLA] Well, I dunno …

NOLA: Could be remembering what to take. Or what to leave. A girlfriend of mine lost some costume jewellery at the Mater.

GIRLIE: [*hissing*] You can't be too careful! You can't call your teeth your own once you get inside a hospital.

NOLA: Mind you, I'm not suggesting that the nuns … There are all sorts that come and go.

GIRLIE: [*craning*] There are all sorts …

MAVIS: Harry, what am I …? The overnight, Harry!

  HARRY *disappears to fetch the bag.*

FIRST MAN: You can relax, Mrs Knott.

  The AMBULANCE MEN *lift her.*

MAVIS: [*tearfully*] My husband …

FIRST MAN: [*taking the weight, grimly*] Ladies are having babies every moment of the day. You'll find it monotonous yourself after the first half-dozen.

  HARRY *reappears with the overnight bag.*

MAVIS: [*to* HARRY] Oh, dear! What are you gunna do? There's the cold mutton …

GIRLIE: [*getting angry*] What are they doing in there?

  The AMBULANCE MEN *emerge, carrying* MAVIS *down the steps.* HARRY *follows with the bag.*

NOLA: [*sucking her teeth*] Poor soul!

  ROY *and* JUDY *move forward, murmuring goodbyes. They touch* MAVIS *as she passes.*

ROY: [*patting her*] See you soon, Mavis.

JUDY: [*bending, softly*] … over … soon … Mrs Knott.

MAVIS: [*protesting*] You're no longer a person. You're a sack!

NOLA: [*calling*] Keeping me fingers crossed, love!

GIRLIE: … any little thing. Just you tell Harry. A cold baked custard … Some of those hospitals leave it all to the relatives and friends.

MAVIS: Oh, dear! Harry? I can feel … I got the—

FIRST MAN: Take it easy, Mrs Knott. Try not to rock the—

HARRY: Here I am, dear. Right beside you. I'm coming in the ambulance.

MAVIS: [*wearily*] I wonder what you're gunna do when that alarm doesn't go off in the morning?

PIPPY: [*calling*] 'Bye, Mrs Knott! We'll come and see the little baby!

> MAVIS *is carried off through the front garden, accompanied by* HARRY. *As this happens,* GIRLIE, PIPPY *and* DEEDREE *run through the front part of the Pogson house.* NOLA *disappears to the front of hers.*

GIRLIE: [*offstage, calling, angrily*] Mind that jardineer, Deedree! You'll have it over!

> JUDY *and* ROY *remain in the centre of the Knott yard.*

JUDY: [*upset*] I'm so sorry for her!

ROY: What's so terrible about the natural occurrences?

JUDY: It's more than that. Can't you see? This house … all of a sudden it's empty. All of a sudden all the little things … that meant something to somebody … don't mean anything anymore. It was the owners who gave them their importance. It's pitiful!

ROY: Possessions!

JUDY: They're part of you till you go. Then they're nothing.

ROY: But can never die right out. Upholstery breeds like man … as often and as ugly.

> *A silence.*

JUDY: [*moodily*] We shall never see anything through each other's eyes.

ROY: Nobody does … really. That doesn't make it tragic.

> *He takes her hand.*

JUDY: [*insisting*] Oh, but they do! Some people do! I'm convinced!

ROY: [*turning her face towards him*] I would like you to see me through your eyes.

JUDY: [*bitterly*] Would you take the risk? Would you dare to be seen as you really are? [*With scorn*] I might even 'possess' you! Then where would you be?

ROY: We'd sort ourselves out in time. Two people have to develop a way to love.

JUDY: [*shaking her head free*] Now it's 'love'! [*Sullenly decided*] I'm not the intellectual type. I couldn't talk to you enough about it.

ROY: If it's a practical demonstration … [*passionately*] I can show you! [*Embracing her*] Convince … you what it is I … need … most!

JUDY: [*fiercely, whispering, between her teeth*] Need! [*Wrenching herself away*] You've worked it out on paper! Along with the notes for the books you never write!

ROY: Can't you believe in lightning?

JUDY: If it struck me dead … then, perhaps, I'd begin to believe in it.

ROY: [*sincerely, gentler*] Darling Judy! [*Again kissing her passionately*] Now I see … know … feel …

JUDY: [*stiffly, from behind closed eyes*] And I … feel … nothing …

> She opens her eyes. He might have intended to caress her, but her manner repels him.

ROY: This is the moment one hopes may never happen!

JUDY: [*sadly*] Once I wanted love. Oh, it seems as though for years … years longer than possible … I've sat around dreaming of nothing else. Somebody to fall in love with. Then I wanted a real person. I wanted you, Roy … [*Turning to him, looking at him, but her manner continues to hold him off.*] Wanting you so badly, I'd almost bang my head against the wall at night. So helpless. Then, quite suddenly … quite recently … was it in the last few minutes …? I found I no longer wanted love.

ROY: [*exasperated*] But … [*laughing*] no one's desirable all of the time!

JUDY: This isn't a question of desire.

ROY: [*flip*] If not … what?

JUDY: It sounds very silly. What is simple … obvious … but true … can be made to sound ridiculous … by clever people.

ROY: Let's have it, though! What's to take the place of this wild beast, which not even you will persuade me to leave off hunting?

> JUDY *scarcely dares.*

JUDY: [*diffidently*] Kindness. Affection. That's all that really matters.

ROY: Kindness? Spaniels!

JUDY: [*unswerving*] Loving kindness!

ROY: That follows. After people have stopped loving. When they've begun to put up with each other.

JUDY: I hope to find it in the beginning. It's more convincing ... valuable ... when it already exists.

> RON SUDDARDS *has entered the Pogson yard from the front garden, rather breathless. He runs up the steps. He is about to knock, but catches sight of* JUDY *and* ROY *in the next yard. He stands looking down at them as they stand looking up.*

RON: [*slowly*] Hello, Judy ... Saw the ambulance turning out of Mildred Street ... Came along to see ...

JUDY: [*answering slowly, coolly*] It was Mrs Knott. She's going to have her baby. Didn't my mother tell you? She was out in front.

RON: Didn't see a soul. The whole street's dead.

> *He appears a little dazed.*

ROY: Excitement dies very quickly. [*Briskly, to* JUDY] Well, I'm going up into this house which you've shown in such a pathetic light ... [*slower*] all emptiness and furniture.

JUDY: [*turning, impulsively*] Oh, Roy, you make me feel I've done and said the most horrible things!

ROY: [*running up the steps, recovering his steely self*] Don't let charity make you do, or say, anything you might regret more. That would be the worst sell of all.

> *He enters the Knott kitchen and crosses it quickly.*

> [*Singing, raucous, in authentic pop tones*] 'You ob-vi-ously do not adore me ...' [*Speaking, very soberly*] Was there any reason why you should?

> ROY *exits into the front part of the house. At the same time* RON *descends the Pogson step.*

RON: [*slowly*] Judy, I interrupted ... something important.

JUDY: [*squeezing through the fence*] No, you didn't, Ron. What you interrupted was nothing. Do you see? Of no importance at all.

> *They look at each other.*

RON: I see.

JUDY: [*approaching him*] I know now ... [*taking his hands*] what I think ... [*holding his hands to her cheek*] you've always known.

RON: [*laughing, softly, happily*] I'm the one should be holding hands!
JUDY: We'll hold each other's … equally.

> *They cling to each other in the shadow of the fence, kissing freely, in joyful relief.* DEEDREE *and* PIPPY *have entered the Pogson kitchen from the front of the house.*

GIRLIE: [*offstage, calling*] Don't you go far now, Joyleen! I've got some things for you to do!
PIPPY: [*calling back, making a face*] May not go anywhere, anyways!
DEEDREE: [*giggly, chanting*] Oily Joyly,
>> Ate a doily.
>> Spewed it up
>> In her cup …

> DEEDREE *continues to giggle inanely at her own wit.*

PIPPY: [*loftily*] That isn't funny.
DEEDREE: 'Tis!
PIPPY: 'Tisn't!

> *They fall silent.*

DEEDREE: [*putting out a feeler*] I got a secret I'll share with you.
PIPPY: What?

> DEEDREE *approaches and whispers to* PIPPY *behind her hand.*

[*Contemptuously*] That's not much of a secret.
DEEDREE: [*whining*] Oh, why?
PIPPY: It's not worth having.
DEEDREE: Why's nothing worth having without you think of it?
PIPPY: Because I have better ideas.

> DEEDREE *drifts wretchedly to the back door.*

DEEDREE: Aren't you coming out, then?
PIPPY: What for?
DEEDREE: Muck around.

> *She looks out, beckoning wildly to* PIPPY, *who acts superior.* DEEDREE *beckons ever more frantically.* PIPPY *cannot resist.* DEEDREE *reveals* RON *and* JUDY.

PIPPY: Oh, that! Thought she was going soft on him.
DEEDREE: That's that Mr Suddards.

PIPPY: Ron Suddards's a drip.
DEEDREE: I think he's nice.
PIPPY: Wears brown socks.

> PIPPY *and* DEEDREE *descend the steps, looking and not looking.*

DEEDREE: Nice colour hair.
PIPPY: Not bad.
DEEDREE: Nice in his sweatshirt.
PIPPY: [*deciding grudgingly*] Mmmmmm.

> *The children prepare to depart for the street, looking back openly now, from the corner of the house.*

She's pretty soppy, though. Isn't she soppy?

> DEEDREE *whispers feverishly to* PIPPY *behind her hand.*

[*Shrieking*] That's different! That's with dogs! And empresses …

> PIPPY *and* DEEDREE *go off towards the street, screaming their heads off.* JUDY *and* RON *have come forward into the centre of the Pogson yard. They have a kind of quiet serenity.*

JUDY: It's so peaceful …
RON: [*tweaking her ear*] Dull is what they call it!
JUDY: In the whole of Sarsaparilla, nobody knows as much as us.
RON: That's how it ought to be for a little.
JUDY: Until we sound a trumpet. [*Becoming more ambitious, visualising, indicating with her hands*] Or masses. Desks and desks! Of massed brass!
RON: [*laughing happily*] Get that old What's-His-Name … that Handel to blow his head off for us. Split the sky open at last. He's the one. He would have been glad …

> *They go off hand in hand, down the lane. At the same time* ERNIE BOYLE *enters the Boyle kitchen. He is sprucely dressed, shaven. He looks at himself gloomily in the wall mirror. Opens his mouth. Makes a despairing face at himself, then stands staring after it has faded.* NOLA *enters. Also dressed for going out, but obviously has not realised* ERNIE *was in the kitchen.*

NOLA: Didn't know you was thinking of going out, Ern.
ERNIE: [*aggressively and defensively*] I wasn't goin' out. Not exactly.

NOLA: You're all dressed up, anyway. Don't often put on your gunmetal flannel.

A pause.

ERNIE: [*more aggressively*] Well, if you'd like to know, I'm gunna drive down to the Bull. Get meself a beer or two.

NOLA: In that suit!

ERNIE: You dress up, don't you, when you're gunna celebrate?

NOLA: [*faintly*] Celebrate?

But ERNIE *does not attempt to explain.*

What are you going to … celebrate?

ERNIE: The day my eyes was well and truly opened.

NOLA *sits down abruptly on the lounge and fetches out her handkerchief. She has grown rather soggy.*

[*Without turning*] And what are you up to? Goin'on the streets?

NOLA *breaks down.*

NOLA: [*crying*] I was going up to Woolie's. Move around a bit. I can't stay here … listening to the clock. A clock in an empty house can send a person barmy.

ERNIE: [*wildly*] Invite some of 'em in, then! Make 'em comfortable in the home! We got the furniture!

NOLA *sits looking at her hands and her miserable handkerchief.*

NOLA: I know about meself, Ern. You don't have to rub it in.

ERNIE: Sometimes it looks as if you don't know. Or perhaps it's just that you forget too often.

NOLA: [*controlling herself*] I think it's best if you go off and get shickered as you planned.

ERNIE: Shickered! That's a nice sort of word for a lady to use!

NOLA: That's a word I learned from my dad, and I used it because no other word says so good what it's supposed to. Dad only used it under provocation, though. He was not one for the booze, or anything else.

ERNIE: He handed on a pretty good line in morals!

NOLA: [*quietly*] Dad's not to blame if I grew up with a blistered heel.

ERNIE: [*ferociously*] Thought it was supposed to be the parents.

NOLA: [*averting her face*] Nobody's going to hold that against us!

There is a silence. ERNIE *suddenly turns away as though he has been slashed. He is trembling. He walks about in great agitation, making inarticulate noises.* NOLA *does not look at him at first.*

[*Not looking at him, blurting*] I didn't suggest that you ... [*Wearily*] We know I'm about as barren as an old boot.

ERNIE *is desperate. He stands in the centre of the stage. He could be about to break down.*

[*Wearily, quietly, going to him, to protect*] Ernie, we seem to 'uv been accusing each other all our lives. And we don't even think of something new!

She reaches him just as he appears to break up. They stand, centre stage, clutching at each other. His head is against her shoulder. He is not exactly crying, but has broken out in a kind of dry rasping.

[*Softly, soothing, a little shocked, though she had half expected it*] Ernie! Ernie!

She caresses him.

ERNIE: [*panting*] It's me that's weak, it seems. I'm the weak one.

NOLA: [*willing him*] No more than most. Ern, dear! D'yer hear? D'you know why I loved you? Because you was never dismal. You always stood up to things better than the others. 'That little fat bugger,' I said, 'he's cheerful. I'm gone on him for that before anything else.'

ERNIE *has quietened, but remains passive in more or less the same position, listening.* NOLA *is warming to the past, or her own performance, or both. The emotional flood is gathering strength.*

So I've always waited. I've waited for you to come in. My life's been set by you, Ern. By your coming in and going out. Even in the days when we had no more than that bloody old black lounge suite that we swapped for the Wilton square, I wouldn't 'uv waited for nobody else. [*On dangerous ground*] Not regular. [*Suddenly bursting into tears*] None of those!

She slides down against him.

I know I'm lost, Ern ... [*kissing his thigh*] but I'd be more lost without you. I'd finish it ... without ...

She grasps his ankles, crying, paddling her hair in his feet. ERNIE *has been wrung dry.*

ERNIE: [*dully*] Better get up, Nola. Somebody might come in.

He tries to free his ankles by motions of the feet.

[*Very stiff*] Go on! That prissy old cow from next door …

NOLA: [*still crying, spasmodically*] She don't need to come in. She was born with imagination. And a thousand ears.

She sits up sniffing. Awful. ERNIE *goes and looks out the back door. He is shattered.*

ERNIE: We both showed up pretty well.

NOLA: D'you know, Ernie, sometimes I lie and watch you when you're asleep. [*Blowing her nose*] There's some men you can't bear to watch when they're sleeping.

She gets up, blowing her nose.

ERNIE: That bloody Masson!

NOLA: I hated him from the start.

ERNIE: So you did.

NOLA: All those mates! The desert gives me the creeps. I wonder what a woman would do in the desert. And those foxholes! All those men … lying in foxholes … and talking about things … [*Fiercely*] I hated all that!

ERNIE: [*sadly*] It's just something that happened in some part of a man's life. If it happened at all …

There is a short silence. ERNIE *walks about, shakily, distracted.* NOLA *looks at herself in the glass.*

NOLA: I've never looked so bloody awful.

ERNIE: [*without looking at her to confirm*] You look awful all right. Like a soddy scone.

NOLA *purses up her mouth in the glass.*

NOLA: Some day it comes to you, they say … to stay …

ERNIE: I'll never believe in that day.

ERNIE *is going towards the door at the back of the stage, tired out.* NOLA *pretends to be intent on making up her mouth.*

NOLA: [*too bright*] What are you gunna do, Ern?

ERNIE: What am I gunna do? I'm gunna get out of this suit. Dressed up like a sore finger …

> ERNIE *exits to the bedroom.* NOLA *buries her face in her hands. She is taking the deep breaths of somebody returning to life.*

[*Offstage, calling*] You might bring that cold bottle. And a couple of glasses. We can sit a while in front.

> NOLA *goes to the fridge. She is exhausted, but wearing an expression of restored happiness.*

NOLA: [*taking the bottle, fetching glasses*] Might as well get undressed meself. Don't know whatever persuaded me I could wear an orange blouse.

> NOLA *exits through the back. Simultaneously* CLIVE POGSON *returns. He enters smartly from his own front garden, carrying the rolled evening paper. Whistling.* GIRLIE POGSON *enters her kitchen.* CLIVE *and* GIRLIE *meet on the steps.*

GIRLIE: Where's the melon?

CLIVE: The melon?

GIRLIE: That we spoke about.

CLIVE: Oh.

> *He hesitates, then goes on in and hangs his hat.*

GIRLIE: You didn't get the melon?

> CLIVE *shoots his cuffs and draws his chin in.*

CLIVE: No.

GIRLIE: When I was relying on the melon!

CLIVE: [*balefully*] Well, I didn't get it. I forgot it. See?

> CLIVE *exits through the back, followed by* GIRLIE, *complaining unintelligibly. At the same time* MR ERBAGE *comes into the Knotts' yard from the street. He is obviously very put out. He runs up the steps pretty briskly for a fat man. Knocks loudly. No reply.*

ERBAGE: [*calling*] Mr Child?

> *He waits. Knocks again.* ROY *enters the kitchen.*

[*Relieved*] Ah, Mr Child … [*but upset*] I came around …

ROY, *all attention, leads* ERBAGE *slowly down into the yard.*

[*Embarrassed*] I came … Something has happened.

ROY: Something in the Council?

ERBAGE: Wish it was! You can manage public affairs. They're open to influence. It's the private ones …

They have arrived at the bottom of the steps.

I've come to advise you re a friend of yours, Mr Child.

ROY: A friend?

ERBAGE: [*mopping himself*] That Miss Julia Sheen.

ROY: I always thought, Mr Erbage, you and she were closely acquainted … not to say connected.

ERBAGE: Not on your life! That is, we were, I suppose, technically.

ROY: Technique should clinch the matter.

ERBAGE: Eh?

ROY: All right. Let it pass.

ERBAGE's anger gets the better of his mystification.

ERBAGE: Look 'ere, I came around for pretty important reasons.

ROY: Yes? Yes? Let's have it.

ERBAGE: Your friend, Miss Julia Sheen, has taken her father's car, and driven it against a wall.

ROY: Good God!

ERBAGE: We hope so. 'Cos the young lady's … passed on.

ROY: [*moved, half to himself*] Then, brittle Julia did break at last.

ERBAGE: [*puzzled*] Eh?

He is sweating at every pore, and mopping constantly.

The point is: there's to be an enquiry. The father's an enquiring man. Who knows who and what will come out of it whole?

ROY: [*genuinely, if not deeply concerned*] Poor Julia! Her legs were perfect.

ERBAGE: I'm not one to disagree that she had what it takes.

ROY: [*prepared for sentimental recapitulation*] Her neck …

ERBAGE: 'Er neck? Yes, it was 'er neck. She can't 'uv known much about it.

Both are silenced for a moment.

ROY: This is horrible! Did you know Julia was expecting a child?

ERBAGE: I did hear something. Something. But Julia was an excitable girl. You might say hysterical.

He looks at ROY *pointedly.*

She might have imagined things. But I won't say more. She's a goner.

ROY: Can't defend herself from her mistakes.

ERBAGE: You've said it! It might have been one. But more likely it was many. [*Looking at* ROY] Eh, Mr Child?

ROY: I wouldn't know. I was never there. [*Looking at* ERBAGE] I should have been, of course. Then none of this might have happened.

ERBAGE: In the circumstances, I don't see who's to blame.

ROY: Everybody is always a little to blame.

ERBAGE: Well, I only thought I'd tip you off. [*Mopping himself again*] A man's reputation can suffer. Particularly in the public service. [*Preparing to leave*] If I can ever do anyone a favour … [*mopping*] it's no trouble, I'm sure.

ERBAGE *is making for the street.*

ROY: [*calling*] Thank you, Mr Erbage, for telling. I'm sorry about the scare you had.

ERBAGE: [*turning*] Eh? Well, I mean to say … I worked pretty hard to get where I got, and it don't seem fair if a little bit of pleasure goes wrong …

ROY: It'll pass. Don't worry, Mr Erbage. We are not the kind that suffer. That's our trouble.

ERBAGE: There, we're coming into country where I've never been before. I never saw the necessity for getting clever. [*Nodding*] Good evening, Mr Child.

ERBAGE *exits through the back. During the foregoing,* CLIVE POGSON *has entered their kitchen from the front part of the house and seated himself with his evening paper.*

CLIVE: [*studying the paper*] Some girl has run herself against a wall. Wonder what gets into them. Suppose the usual. You're up against that sort of thing with girls. [*Thoughtfully*] Now if we had had boys … [*More cheerfully*] But boys don't pay when the parents grow old. A girl will bring you a billy of soup …

HARRY KNOTT *has entered the Pogson yard from the street. He is very tired, but satisfied. He climbs the steps, is about to knock, but catches sight of* CLIVE.

HARRY: I passed by, Mr Pogson … thought you might like to know …

CLIVE: [*coming to the door, lethargically*] Yairs, Harry?

HARRY: It's a boy, Mr Pogson.

CLIVE: I'm real glad! It's a satisfaction to have a boy.

HARRY: [*sighing*] I'll say!

CLIVE: She was quick, though.

HARRY: [*as he turns away*] Oh, I got a taxi home.

CLIVE: [*watching his neighbour*] I'll tell the wife … [*slower, quieter, frowning at the front rooms*] tell the wife …

CLIVE *re-seats himself with his paper.* HARRY *goes on through the fence, catching sight of* ROY.

HARRY: It's a boy, Roy.

ROY: [*sympathetically, but absent*] I'm glad, Harry. It had to be.

HARRY *goes up the steps. Very exhausted.*

HARRY: She told me something … something I had to do …

HARRY *exits towards the front rooms.*

ROY: So they die. So they are born. And are the sins of the watchers forgiven, in the backyards, at dusk?

ROY *exits down the lane. At the same time* ERNIE *and* NOLA *enter their kitchen.* ERNIE *is wearing his work clothes, carrying his coat.* NOLA *is comfortable in her usual chenille dressing-gown.*

NOLA: Have to get you a bit of tea.

ERNIE: Nah.

NOLA: But you gotta eat.

ERNIE: I feel good. I feel warm.

He kisses hungrily—bite-kisses—down her neck.

I ate!

NOLA: [*giggling, withdrawing*] You're a trimmer! You'll leave bruises for everyone to see.

ERNIE: Trademarks.

NOLA: [*serious, drawing her gown close*] But wrap up warm, Ern. One of those southerlies come. I felt it as we were laying on top of the bed.

ERNIE: [*putting on his coat*] You don't have time to feel cold.

NOLA: [*laughing*] Don't get yarning to all those ladies! In the small hours. In the homes.

ERNIE *starts feeling his coat.*

ERNIE: 'Ere, what's all this?

NOLA: What?

ERNIE: Me coat?

NOLA: I gave it to the dry cleaners.

ERNIE: Me old coat!

NOLA: We agreed, didn't we? We agreed to give it to the gentleman who's started calling regular with the van.

ERNIE: Didn't know …

NOLA: Well, we did. [*After a pause*] He's ever so polite.

ERNIE *is listening.*

D'you know … that man's wife has had eleven operations. She's had practically the whole of her insides taken away from her. She's practically all plastic now.

ERNIE: [*gloomily*] She would be.

Another pause.

NOLA: [*laughing*] He's a funny sort of bloke.

ERNIE: [*gloomier*] 'Ow?

NOLA: Oh, I dunno. He's red. [*Shuddering*] Ugh, I don't like the red, freckly men!

ERNIE: Don't go much on the blueys meself.

He goes out down the steps, thoughtful, and sad.

NOLA: [*calling*] Aren't you gunna kiss me?

ERNIE: [*looking back*] I did!

NOLA: [*giggling, softly*] That's right! You did!

ERNIE *goes on, turns again, and waves, but sad.* NOLA *blows him a couple of fruity kisses. He turns for the last time, then exits down the lane.* NOLA *sighs, withdrawn inside the kitchen, rubbing her arms.*

[*Sighing*] Ah, dear! Pippy was right. It's lonely when you're on your own. What can you do? Look at the TV … [*Grimacing*] A lot of grey tadpoles …

NOLA *exits into the front of the house.* ROY *has entered from the lane. He has returned to the Knott yard and is standing against the proscenium arch in his characteristic attitude for observing.*

ROY: In Mildred Street there's practically no end to the variations on monotony. The Iceland poppies replace the glads, the dahlias take their turn with the chrysanths. At weekends, Pogsons are painting their house a shade of French Grey they've seen on someone else's. Boyles are indulging in a daring splash of red. Nothing stands still. Not in the razzle-dazzle of time.

Razzle-dazzle is turned on.

People are spattered and splashed by it, of course. But for the most part, not very dangerously. So the men of Mildred Street continue on their way … out, in … in, out …

HARRY *and* CLIVE *march out through the razzle-dazzle of light, dressed for business, as* ERNIE *returns from work via the lane. All greet one another—conventional gestures—as the commentary continues.* HARRY *and* CLIVE *exit through the back.* ERNIE *enters his kitchen and exits to the unseen rooms.*

Supported by Hire Purchase, the splendid climate, and their Australian extrovert temperament, they are able to lead the Good Life. Some of them have even sent the population up …

MAVIS *enters her kitchen and is hanging out nappies.*

My sister Mavis has been home … is it two … three … how many weeks? She had her boy easily enough, and for some unknown reason chose to call him … Kev-on. Mavis is the cornucopia. Mavis must spill, and in that find her purpose, her contentment.

JUDY *and* RON *have entered the Pogson yard by way of the lane. They are holding hands, courting. They moon around the yard.*

Here's my girl, Judy Pogson. She seems to have struck it pretty good. Whether she's struck the best, only time, that lovely and distorting razzle-dazzle, will show … as the price of things goes up, but never down … as the men of Mildred Street continue marching … in, out … out, in … through the sunny Australian climate, and the rain of politicians' promises …

> CLIVE *and* HARRY *re-enter from the back.* ERNIE *enters his kitchen from the inner rooms, followed by* NOLA. CLIVE *and* HARRY *step inside their homes as* ERNIE *leaves his. Conventional greetings.* NOLA *stands and waves.*

The sanitary man's wife is sad. She's between her times. Something has ended, and nothing has begun.

> NOLA *turns back into her kitchen.* GIRLIE *enters hers.* HARRY *and* CLIVE *exit through the back, after kissing their wives.* ERNIE *exits down the lane.* JUDY *and* RON *have seated themselves on the Pogson steps, absorbed in each other.* MAVIS *and* GIRLIE *busy themselves at their stoves with conventional gestures.* NOLA *has seated herself on the lounge, looking through a magazine, licking her thumb liberally from time to time.*

MAVIS: Food, food …

GIRLIE: … food is always the question …

NOLA: … meals to shove in front of men.

GIRLIE: Steak, chops, chops, steak …

NOLA: Meat is a must for men … with the juice running out … and a nice piece of fat to get their tongues around.

MAVIS: Eggs are livery in the end.

GIRLIE: I always say: Educate them in daintiness. A nice spaghetti on toast. Or beans. All this meat! They'll complain at first. But settle down. Daintiness pays …

ROY: … and food is so nourishing. Not to say necessary. How else to resist being blinded by the razzle-dazzle of time?

> *Razzle-dazzle gives way to normal evening light.* ROY *goes up into the Knotts' house.* CLIVE *and* HARRY *have come out into their respective kitchens. The wives serve their husbands with food.*

HARRY: [*to* MAVIS] Would you say they were grey, or blue?

MAVIS: [*without hesitation*] Oh, blue! There's no mistaking when he opens them at you.

> HARRY *and* MAVIS *are too absorbed to notice* ROY, *who passes them and exits to the rooms beyond.*

RON: [*to* JUDY, *as they sit looking into each other*] You know, when I first met you, I thought your eyes were blue. Then I saw they were grey.

JUDY: [*laughing*] They're really a kind of dirty green.

Pause, as they continue looking at each other.

[*Gently touching his eyes*] There's no mistaking brown. Brown eyes are for faithfulness.

PIPPY *has entered the Pogson kitchen from the bedrooms. She sits at the table with a book. Absorbed.* NOLA *hums and vibrates, looking through her magazine.* CLIVE *pauses in his eating.*

CLIVE: [*looking out through the doorway*] It's a lovely evening all right.

GIRLIE: When I was a girl, at Rosedale, oh, the evenings were lovely then! Playing rummy on the mosquito-proof verandah. With the young fellers who would come in. Off the neighbouring properties. Oh, the light beneath the willows! Oh, the lamplight at Rosedale, when I was a girl!

CLIVE: Yairs. Rosedale! We know all about that.

NOLA's *humming stops. She throws aside the magazine. She sits with her face cupped in her hands, staring out into the evening.*

NOLA: Perhaps if I had a cat. A little, white, fluffy cat …

GIRLIE: [*to* CLIVE] It's peaceful enough in Mildred Street. Nowadays, at least. Remember all those dogs? How disgraceful! I'll never forget. Anyway, it's finished.

PIPPY: [*raising her head*] But it's gunna begin again.

CLIVE *and* GIRLIE *look at her aghast.*

CLIVE and GIRLIE: [*together*] When?

PIPPY: In six months time.

GIRLIE: [*almost crying*] But it shouldn't be allowed!

PIPPY: Every six months. For ever and ever.

CLIVE: How d'you know all this, Pippy?

PIPPY: Mrs … [*Thinking better of it, cold and superior*] I learned it.

She turns away to her book.

MAVIS: [*to* HARRY] The whole thing with a baby is to give it affection. I read that in a magazine. Look, when little Kevon—

ROY *enters from the front part of the house. He is carrying a pack.* MAVIS *and* HARRY *both notice him this time, and stare.*

HARRY: What's … what's got into you, Roy?

ROY: I'm going away.

MAVIS: You never said you was going away.

HARRY: What, up the coast somewhere?

MAVIS: Some say the air's nicer down the south.

ROY: No. I'm going away … London … Paris … the Galapagos Islands … It doesn't much matter where.

MAVIS: [*laughing*] Aren't you a caution?! Send us a postcard, then. [*Recovering her real interest*] Look, I was telling Harry tonight, you'd never guess what that kid did. When I went in after his sleep, he looked at me … and winked, Roy!

HARRY: [*pushing back his plate*] You can tell that kiddy's got a sense of humour even now …

> ROY *continues out.*

ROY: 'Bye, Mavis. 'Bye, Harry.

> But MAVIS *and* HARRY *have forgotten about him. So he continues slowly down the steps.*

MAVIS: Look, Harry, I tell you who he's like. It isn't Dad after all. It's my Uncle Will. A big, happy sort of man …

> A desperate outburst of humming from NOLA, *as she sits tossing the slipper on her toes.*

GIRLIE: [*to* PIPPY] But I shan't be able to stand it again!

PIPPY: [*beating time remorselessly with her head*] Over, and over, and over. For ever, and ever, and ever. That's nature!

> ROY *has reached the lane. He stands at the centre of the stage.*

ROY: [*looking back at the rear view Mildred Street*] Listen to them, the poor sods! They'll still be at it when I get back … [*Slower, more thoughtful*] Because … of course … I shall get back. [*Exasperated*] You can't shed your skin even if it itches like hell!

> He goes off down the lane, as if to avoid emotion by a speedy departure. The lights dim. When they go up again, the other characters have removed themselves.

THE END

.